WITHDRAWN

PACKAGING
Makeovers

ROCKPORT

PACKAGING
Makeovers

graphic redesign for market change

GLOUCESTER MASSACHUSETTS

ROCKPORT PUBLISHERS

Stacey King Gordon

First published in the United States of America by
Rockport Publishers, Inc.
33 Commercial Street
Gloucester, Massachusetts 01930-5089
Telephone: (978) 282-9590
Fax: (978) 283-2742

Library of Congress Cataloging-in-Publication Data available

ISBN 1-59253-110-5

10 9 8 7 6 5 4 3 2

Cover Design: Rockport Publishers
Cover Images: Main image: Malcolm Robertson
          Front (left top, middle, and bottom): Clinton Hussey
          Back (right): Eduardo Fuentes Osorio
Page Design and Layout: Art & Anthropology

Printed in China

Many thanks to the wise and talented designers and creative directors who contributed their vision to this project. Also, my gratitude to Kristin Ellison for her infinite patience and guidance. And, thanks to Andrew for rooting me on, during this project and always.

Contents

Introduction

To say packaging designers are busy people these days is a colossal understatement—and much of their work involves the refreshing, evolution, or complete overhaul of existing product packaging already on the shelf.

These days, it's not unusual for a major consumer brand to require a packaging change every two years. And because it typically takes that long for an international brand's packaging design to permeate all corners of the world, by the time the new package is finally on every retail shelf, it's time to start all over again.

Why such a rigorous routine? There are, of course, the obvious reasons. Consumers have more choices in the market than ever. New generations of consumers expect and demand different things. And these days, 80 percent of a consumer's decision is now made at the shelf, with an emphasis more on first impressions and price than on brand reputation and purchasing history.

"Loyalty is diminishing, and a lot of it has to do with the emergence of store brands, which are cheaper and widely perceived to be good," says Scott Young, president of Perception Research Services in Fort Lee, New Jersey, a firm that conducts more than 500 customer-research studies a year to help brands understand their standing in the marketplace. "Given the price gap, it is important for national brands to make sure that their packaging helps to justify the price premium. Now that store brands are doing a better job with their packaging, it drives national brands to innovate and reach the next level."

Of course, any kind of change when it comes to packaging is a dangerous proposition. Marketing managers can measure, analyze, and hypothesize all they want, but gauging consumers' emotional connections to a brand's look—and predicting their response to a redesign—is a tenuous science. Many times, companies prefer to hover close to the original look, embarking on an evolutionary change that freshens up the package without altering its legacy impression. In other situations, the redesign is more revolutionary—holding tight to a few important equity elements but tossing out the rest and beginning anew.

This book categorizes the featured projects by reason for redesign—a key premise, because the ultimate decision about the design approach varies, depending on the original package's main flaw:

- It needs an up-to-date tweaking
- It's out-and-out ineffective
- It's flailing against the competition
- It must accommodate a new focus for the product

Beyond these four basic reasons, more complex forces drive companies to reconsider their packaging—its shelf impact, its "line logic" or system architecture, its information design, and its structure—on an ongoing basis. The same forces also have a strong influence on companies' design decisions. A few of these reasons include:

Changing Retail Channels

The prominence of retail superstores changes everything. "It's not just about the packaging experience—it's about the entire retail experience," says Eric Weissinger of Fitch Worldwide in Columbus, Ohio. Package designers must consider how a box will look when stacked with dozens of other boxes to create a "billboard" effect, especially if the primary retail space is a warehouse or big-box store where products are merchandised in the middle of the floor instead of on a shelf. Plus, superstores aren't known for their experienced and knowledgeable staff. "Consumers expect innovation, and the packaging has to sell itself," Weissinger says.

Evolving Industries

Ten years ago, inkjet printers were marketed as an inexpensive way to get minimal print quality for text documents at home. Now, the market has become all about imaging. With the increasing popularity of digital cameras, more people expect inkjets that can print photo-quality photos. Therefore, the brands that sell printer technology must become more imaging centered. As an industry evolves, the packaging for the products needs to tell a different story to strike a nerve with consumers.

Shifting Consumer Bases

The best example of a shifting consumer base is the changing target audience for Home Depot. Not long ago, contractors and suburban husbands with a honey-do list shopped there. Now, 50 percent of the retailer's shoppers are women, inspired by home-improvement magazines and cable channels. Products must not only appeal to female consumers but must also be accessible enough for all DIYers to buy them. In many categories, companies are rethinking what they've always taken as truth when it comes to the primary audience for their products.

Globalization

As companies expand their reach, they recognize the impact of an internationally strong brand—a brand that is resolutely consistent in every market in the world. Many companies are moving from a phased and regionally focused approach to a simultaneous global rollout when launching new products, which means they must redesign their packaging to accommodate every manufacturing base's common needs and culture's consumer biases.

Private-Brand Revolution

As consumers become increasingly both price conscious and quality conscious, retail stores' private labels are becoming more important than ever—a development that changes the landscape on both sides of the fence. Manufacturers of national brands scramble to stay several steps ahead of the retailers' private-label products, which are often designed to mimic the branded equivalent. On the retailers' side, the me-too approach is testing as less and less reputable with consumers; therefore, more retailers aim to design a private brand and accompanying packaging that is attractive and unique, such as Target's upscale Archer Farms food brand.

Add all these factors together, and you've got a complex mix driving—and complicating—packaging redesigns. Companies and their design teams must consider the dramatically changing markets that they serve, all while ensuring that the packaging they relaunch maintains a continuous emotional connection with consumers.

This book profiles thirty-three projects in which the designers successfully juggled the extenuating factors and produced refreshes that got results. From small companies on tight budgets to international corporations more than a century old, the clients all had one thing in common: they needed a new face to the world that was perfectly balanced between safely stepping forward and shaking things up. Packaging redesign is part science, part intuition, and part intimate knowledge of how consumers think. But the real success stories are the designs that rely on a little magic—the mysterious formula that excites, entices, and, in the end, makes the sale.

A New Sales Pitch:
MANUFACTURER CHANGE OF FOCUS

before

The old Adobe Acrobat packaging had been on the shelves for three years. Although the running man on the front was a familiar icon for the software, other elements of the graphics, including the soft pastels and the geographic inferences (showing the man leaping from New York to Paris), limited the product in terms of scope and impact.

In just three weeks, PrimoAngeli:Fitch designed a packaging system that put a new face on the revolutionary new Adobe Acrobat—a product launch that took the tech world by storm.

Adobe Acrobat Design Process

Adobe Acrobat 5.0 had been on the shelf for three years. With this version, most users could download a free Acrobat Reader to open and print PDFs; business users and designers could upgrade to a paid full version that allowed them to create and edit PDFs. As user needs became more complex, however, Adobe decided to launch a line of products that would be even more sophisticated and that would offer professional users a higher-end version with more powerful features, including the ability to route a document for review and systematically collect comments and edits from reviewers.

Adobe Acrobat revolutionized the idea of universally readable file formats. In the days before other software companies had figured out the importance of being able to trade, read, and edit files across platforms and versions, Acrobat PDFs were compact, readable, and printable on practically any PC around the globe.

REASON FOR REDESIGN
Unlike previous versions, Adobe Acrobat 6.0 would be divided into three distinct tiers, requiring a more deliberate packaging architecture. In addition, Adobe's packaging firm PrimoAngeli:Fitch realized the new version represented a significant step forward in the program's capabilities. Therefore, the redesign needed to reflect a new era for Adobe Acrobat.

REDESIGN OBJECTIVES
- Build a packaging system with three tiers that clearly symbolize the levels of functionality
- Retain Adobe Acrobat's brand equities, while communicating the power and evolution of the new version
- Play up the idea of collaboration—the main feature of the new Acrobat—in the package graphics

THE RESULTS
The packaging redesign, combined with the product's new functionality, caused a stir in the market after its launch. In fact, the *New York Times* reported that when Adobe released its sales figures for Acrobat 6.0, they were so positive that they sparked an overall rally in the tech stock sector.

2

3

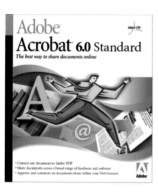

4

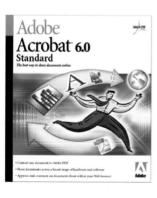

5

6

1
Because the running man icon was so strong, PrimoAngeli:Fitch and Adobe agreed that though he should remain the software's mascot, he needed to be modernized. The graphics needed to enforce the idea of multifaceted communication and full-circle delivery. The designers began sketching ideas for graphical ways to relay that point to consumers.

2
Struck in beta testing by just how far the software program had come since its last release, PrimoAngeli:Fitch knew the packaging, including the product's icon, needed to reflect technological advancement. An on-staff illustrator began developing an Acrobat character that was more hard edged. Another challenge, due to Acrobat's strong market presence around the world, was making the character look as if he could belong to any ethnic group and working around cultural sensitivities.

3
In early comps, designers took the original running man character out of his element and displayed him alongside cyclones of business documents and features.

4
The software's new rollout needed to appeal not only to urban professionals but also to companies located in little villages in China or towns in the American Midwest. The designers removed the running man from his literal city-to-city leap and placed him in a more abstract background. In this interpretation, they show him bounding through colorful symbols of software features—type, email, graphics, and data.

5
The final, and eventually selected, direction placed the man against a digitally themed background, with specific depictions of functionality for each packaging tier.

6
In the final designs, Elements 6.0 shows a straight arrow to indicate one-to-one delivery of PDFs. The Standard and Professional versions show the juggling of many different icons across one arched arrow, with a "return" arrow running across the bottom, to symbolize full document circulation. The tiers' colors are also chosen deliberately—for instance, the royal purple tones and golden globe represent the high-end version of the product.

Balducci's

DESIGN
Pearlfisher, London, United Kingdom
MARKET
United States
(New York and Washington, DC metro areas)

Sutton Place Group owned three different brands that were strong and long standing: Sutton Place Gourmet, Balducci's, and Hay Day Country Farm Market. Each brand's logo graced shopping bags and private labels throughout each retail chain, making the logos highly visible to the loyal shoppers.

The final rollout of private-label Balducci's products presented a colorful, unique, and fun-loving packaging system that quickly summed up the contents of each container.

Balducci's Design Process

Having begun in 1980 as a small gourmet food store in Washington, DC, Sutton Place Gourmet quickly grew to a chain of specialty supermarkets throughout the metropolitan area. The holding company that owned Sutton Place Gourmet acquired two other well-known East Coast food brands in the 1990s, Hay Day Country Farm Market and Balducci's. With these acquisitions, Sutton Place Group LLC then owned eleven specialty supermarkets and six restaurants in Virginia, Maryland, the District of Columbia, New York, and Connecticut—prestigious destinations for urban food lovers.

In late 2003, the group announced it would adopt the best-recognized name from its restaurant group—Balducci's—as the brand for all of its properties. The mission of the chain was to create a group of full-service neighborhood supermarkets in the New York City and Washington, DC, areas that offer a range of specialty foods from around the world, superior-quality perishables, and everyday products at affordable prices.

REASON FOR REDESIGN

The former Balducci's was a high-priced specialty Italian food store. The Sutton Place Group wanted to shed this image in favor of positioning Balducci's as "the ultimate food lover's market." The group hired Pearlfisher, a firm with offices in London and New York, to redesign its brand identity and execute this into a variety of applications to give Balducci's a new, more distinctive, and universal image.

REDESIGN OBJECTIVES

- Combine three existing brands into a single, universal brand that balances tradition with a modern image, plus demonstrate how the identity could adapt to signage, a full line of private label products, shopping bags, print advertising, store environment
- Develop a clean, simple, accessible look to reflect and promote the new positioning of Balducci's stores, along with an interesting visual and verbal identity that communicates an element of fun and love for food
- Eliminate some of the "negative equity" that the old, high-priced brand had built up in favor of an image that welcomes a range of consumers

THE RESULTS

Consumers responded well to the new name and look of the Balducci's brand—a pleasant surprise for the client, who was initially worried about the reaction from loyal customers.

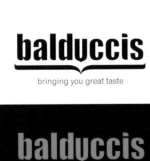

bringing you great taste

1

2

3

4

6

5

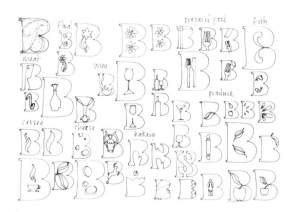

7

8

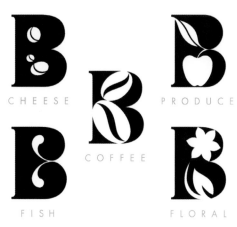

9

10

1, 2
Pearlfisher was given the task of finding a single look that could be applied to everything—shopping bags, packaging, signage, ads, uniforms, and interior design—across the rebranded Balducci's stores. The designers explored several different permutations for visually communicating the theme of "simply loving food." In these comps, designers latched onto the "simple" part of the equation, repeating a single design element—the bracket and the uniquely shaped *b*—for subtle flair in otherwise spare designs.

3
In this exploration, designers played out the literal concept of "loving." The letter *b* with a heart-shaped counter is laid over lusciously colorful images of food.

4, 5
The client ultimately chose the script *B* as the final direction, balancing an element of tradition with modernity.

6–8
One of Pearlfisher's biggest challenges was creating an identity that could be adapted across various applications, from bags to wrapping paper to uniforms. The black-and-white logo remained flexible enough that designers could scale it back (such as on the brown bags shown here) or dress it up (on fancier bags) to take advantage of the full impact of positive and negative space.

9, 10
To create a fun image and a strong emotional connection to the brand, Pearlfisher then embarked on designing a personality for each product category in the store—which includes more than 1,000 different private label products, from coffee to flowers to fish to dairy. The designers sketched out ways to visually represent each category within the familiar black *B*.

Bosque-Lya was an El Salvador sweetheart—a coffee grown, roasted, and produced in the Los Naranjos region west of San Salvador—but the brand wasn't distinctive in name, taste, or look. A busy label layered pretty berries, textured text, and an illustration of the brand's bird mascot that blended in with the background. The label, which was confusing and unreadable, didn't narrate the real story behind the coffee brand.

Café de Lya

DESIGN
Ideas Frescas, San Salvador, El Salvador

ART DIRECTOR
Frida Larios

CONCEPT/DESIGN
Gabriela Larios

COPYWRITERS
Frida Larios and Alejandro Kravetz

MARKET
El Salvador and the United States (expanding into Europe)

The design used offset printing on a canister that kept the coffee fresher and presented a sleek new face to consumers.

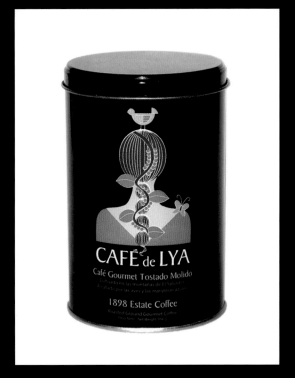

Café de Lya Design Process

For more than forty years, a family-owned business in San Salvador called Sweet's El Palacio de los Postres (which translates to "Sweet's Palace of Desserts") — has been celebrated as a favorite El Salvador bakery. Among the products that the business wanted to begin exporting was a line of coffee called Bosque-Lya, named for Lya de Castañeda, the business's founder and manager of her own coffee plantation. Though it had a strong tradition, the new generation of owners knew they had to improve the quality of the coffee brand before directing it to international markets.

REASON FOR REDESIGN

The Bosque-Lya brand as it stood wasn't strongly affiliated with a recognized set of values and an established identity. The manufacturer wanted to capture the interest of international distributors, especially as a coffee grown and roasted in El Salvador, a country that lost its foothold as a leading coffee producer due to a twelve-year civil war and is currently trying to regain its place among gourmet coffee brands. The coffee needed to stand out with a unique story and distinctive flavor by showing the true values of the brand. Sweet's and its branding and design consultancy, Ideas Frescas, decided that in addition to changing the coffee itself, they wanted to return to the coffee's roots.

REDESIGN OBJECTIVES

• Rebrand the coffee as Café de Lya, a distinctive, memorable, and competitive brand to appeal to international markets
• Rediscover and communicate the coffee's, and the company's, true identity
• Represent a new "gourmet" product

THE RESULTS

In the first months after the relaunch, Café de Lya became the first gourmet coffee brand to be sold in Dutch supermarket giant Royal Ahold's local El Salvador chain, Hiper Paiz, and distributors in the United States have begun ordering the product.

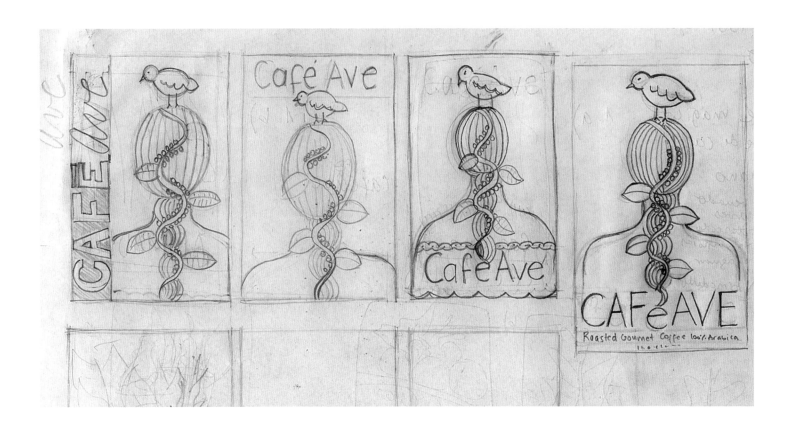

1

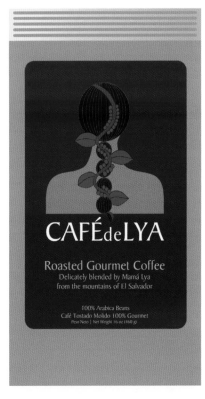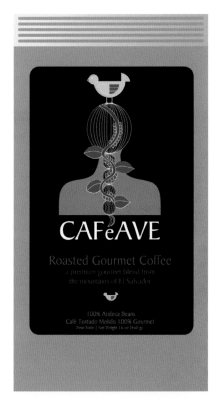

2

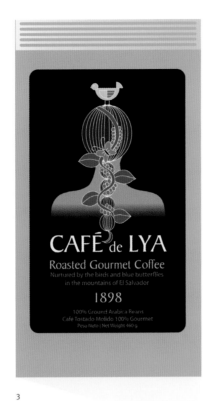

3

4

Branding consultancy Ideas Frescas worked with the coffee's manufacturer to study the heart of the product. The team reached the conclusion that the brand's real draw was its family tradition and its ecological values. The owners' grandmother, Lya de Castañeda, founded the coffee brand, so the designers went down the path of including her spirit on the package as an earthy feminine image. Based on the brand's familiar bird, they explored renaming the brand Café Ave (bird coffee). They also looked to the product's heritage, eventually choosing the name Café de Lya.

2
Original comps incorporated some of the elements from the old packaging—the berries and the bird—but invoked a more feminine, Mother Earth feeling. The designers wanted to reference the flora and fauna that inhabited the tropical forest, from where the gourmet coffee blossomed. "We felt there was a mystic and magical nature in all the process," says art director Frida Larios.

3
The designers and the client labored over every detail of the packaging: typography, text spacing, punctuation, colors, and textures. Even the clothes Lya wore were in question, because of discomfort over the amount of skin the woman should show.

4
The final label used an all-black background with rich, jewel-tone and earthy colors. It complemented the brand's slogan: Grown in the mountains of El Salvador. Nurtured by birds and blue butterflies.

Ciao Bella

DESIGN
Wallace Church, New York, New York
MARKET
United States

Ciao Bella's former packaging was not aimed at consumers at all—it was food-service packaging simply meant to get the product from the factory to the restaurant deep freezer. When the company decided to make a push for consumer sales, it needed a new design for its pints of gelato, sorbet, and frozen yogurt.

The pints, sold in upscale food markets, are too bright, quirky, and fun to miss—and the bold design embodies the quality and innovation of the icy treats within.

Ciao Bella Design Process

Ciao Bella started out twenty years ago as a tiny gelato shop in New York City's Little Italy and grew by word of mouth into an in-demand supplier of gourmet gelato and sorbet to some 1,500 gourmet restaurants around the country. The handmade treats incorporate inventive and exquisite ingredients such as Tahitian vanilla, Belgian chocolate, fresh fruit, spices, and imported Italian flavorings—formulas that discriminating chefs can't resist.

REASON FOR REDESIGN

The company also dabbled in retail, but the owners wanted to expand their reach more broadly into retail to complement its thriving food-service business. Ciao Bella packaging, which had been focused strictly on the trade market, was little more than a white carton with black lettering. To develop a presence in the natural food markets where the company planned to sell the products, Ciao Bella hired Wallace Church, a strategic brand imagery and package design consultancy in New York.

REDESIGN OBJECTIVES

- Design graphics for the company's new pint containers that were as unique, exciting, and innovative as the products themselves
- Create a packaging system and structure to accommodate the constantly growing number of fun flavors
- Help the emerging consumer brand stand out next to the category leaders, Nestle and Unilever, as well as look at home among gourmet and natural food brands in upscale retail environments

THE RESULTS

The results have been very good since the August 2003 launch. In fact, according to Ciao Bella cofounder and CEO F. W. Pearce, sales have nearly doubled since the company began marketing to consumers.

1

LEMON FRUIT ICE

sorbetto

CIAO **CB** BELLA

1 PINT
(473ml)

VANILLA

gelato

CIAO **CB** BELLA

1 PINT
(473ml)

2

LEMON FRUIT ICE

CIAO BELLA GELATO CO. INC.

CIAO
cb
BELLA

EST 1983

FINE ICE CREAMS & SORBETS

sorbetto

1 PINT
(473ml)

VANILLA

CIAO BELLA GELATO CO. INC.

CIAO
cb
BELLA

EST 1983

FINE ICE CREAMS & SORBETS

gelato

1 PINT
(473ml)

3

LEMON FRUIT ICE

CIAO BELLA

SORBETTO

1 PINT
(473ml)

VANILLA

CIAO BELLA

GELATO

1 PINT
(473ml)

4

LEMON FRUIT ICE

CIAO BELLA

FINEST ICE CREAMS & SORBETS

CIAO BELLA GELATO CO. INC.

SORBETTO

1 PINT
(473ml)

COCONUT

CIAO BELLA

FINEST ICE CREAMS & SORBETS

CIAO BELLA GELATO CO. INC.

SORBETTO

1 PINT
(473ml)

PASSION FRUIT & ORANGE

CIAO BELLA

FINEST ICE CREAMS & SORBETS

CIAO BELLA GELATO CO. INC.

SORBETTO

1 PINT
(473ml)

MANGO

CIAO BELLA

FINEST ICE CREAMS & SORBETS

CIAO BELLA GELATO CO. INC.

SORBETTO

1 PINT
(473ml)

5

CIAO BELLA

FINEST ICE CREAMS & SORBETS

CIAO BELLA GELATO CO. INC.

CHEF'S SELECTION
GELATO

CIAO BELLA

FINEST ICE CREAMS & SORBETS

CIAO BELLA GELATO CO. INC.

CHEF'S SELECTION
SORBETTO

CHEF'S SELECTION

CIAO BELLA

FINEST ICE CREAMS & SORBETS

CIAO BELLA GELATO CO. INC.

CHEF'S SELECTION
GELATO

1 PINT
(473ml)

CHEF'S SELECTION

CIAO BELLA

FINEST ICE CREAMS & SORBETS

CIAO BELLA GELATO CO. INC.

CHEF'S SELECTION
SORBETTO

1 PINT
(473ml)

6

1
To create the new visual brand for Ciao Bella, the designers at Wallace Church experimented with many ideas, all based on fun, unique color combinations and shapes. In this comp, X-ray images of the products' main ingredients against a black background call attention to the products' natural origins and lend a more upscale look.

2, 3
These designs keep the black background but opt for brighter, more abstract shapes to provide eye-catching contrast.

4, 5
The bright colors were working, especially because they embodied the brand's innovative spirit and unique flair. Designers explored color combinations and symbols that would best suit the front of the pint cartons.

6
The design finally selected features simple but striking symbols of the product inside: a C-shaped swirl for the gelato and a snowflake for the sorbet. Contrasting, but harmonious, product colors were selected as pairings for the product families.

Dole Fruit Bowls

DESIGN
Addis, Berkeley, California
MARKET
United States

before

Dole had long targeted mothers who buy snacks for their children. The old packaging incorporated some playfulness to that end, with its images of falling fruit and bouncing type. When the company discovered that the mothers—and other women in their peer group—were, in fact, buying the fruit for themselves, Dole knew its packaging needed to address these female consumers looking for healthy alternatives. The company also wanted a more unique, ownable look.

The redesigned package is powerful and moving on the shelf, with mouth-watering images and clearly labeled packaging that leave no question about freshness and healthfulness in the minds of busy women

Dole Fruit Bowls Design Process

In 1999, fruit company Dole Packaged Foods in Westlake Village, California, introduced a product aimed at capturing part of the growing grab-and-go market. Dole Fruit Bowls offered several varieties of healthy snacks in plastic bowls with peel-off lids. When the product first launched, it was designed to appeal to kids—and their moms who shopped for them—as a lunch box snack. The company actually promoted the 4-ounce (113 g) bowls as having dual purposes: Once the kids finished their healthy snacks, they could use the sturdy bowls to plant seeds or collect coins.

REASON FOR REDESIGN

Three years after Fruit Bowls hit the shelves, Dole learned through market research that their target audience was not what they had expected. Though moms with kids were still a significant demographic, the largest group of consumers for Fruit Bowls was single women ages 25 to 35.

Dole decided to reposition the product with an aim for 25- to 45-year-old women, with or without families, who led busy lives and had a difficult time eating well despite their best intentions. New packaging was needed to address this older audience searching for a healthy, convenient snack.

REDESIGN OBJECTIVES

- Target on-the-go adult women who are looking for ways to eat well and naturally but are limited on time
- Exceed previous packaging's on-shelf impact, image of quality and freshness, and system of classifying product varieties
- Create a proprietary style that reflects the Dole brand and sets Fruit Bowls apart from other fruit-based snacks

THE RESULTS

The new look, with its oversized images of fresh fruit, is stopping fast-moving women consumers in their tracks and is carving a special niche in the grab-and-go aisle. The company has seen favorable market response to the new, unique look.

1

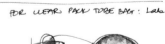

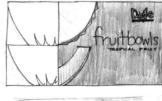

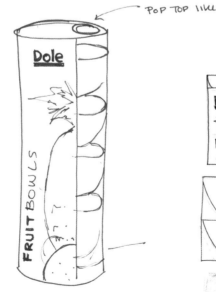

2

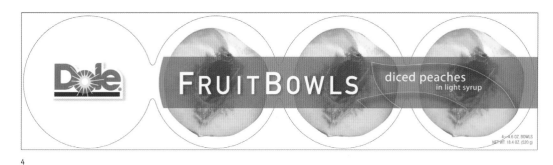

4

3

6

1, 2
Dole wasn't sure how far it wanted to go with its redesign, so design firm Addis set out to explore a range of possible directions, reflecting everything from a complete change in focus to more evolutionary approaches. Initial sketches reveal a revived focus on Fruit Bowls' fresh ingredients, as well as the possibility of a more innovative physical structure for the package.

3, 4
The fresh-approach concept (3) conjured up images of freshness and great taste on a unique, cylindrical package. The fresh-spirit direction (4) also experimented with an innovative new packaging structure—a clear package that evoked a light, pure feel suggesting wellness for the mind, body, and spirit.

5
Some concepts were emotionally based. The fresh-attitude approach featured abstract representations of the fruit for a bright, modern, and sophisticated design approach that was still friendly and accessible.

6
Other concepts, such as fresh view, targeted the senses. The package backlit thinly sliced fruit to allow its natural texture to shine through, a compelling summary of the product's fresh, intense taste.

7
A more evolutionary approach retained the original packaging's playfulness but added a sense of depth and dimensionality to the floating fruit.

8
The concept finally selected by the client was the direction Addis termed "fresh picked:" rich photographic images of whole pieces of succulent fruit, conveying a sense of right-off-the-tree freshness.

5

7

8

Secrets of Success

A change of focus can encompass anything from extending the brand to a complete change in product formula or content. However sweeping the change is, the accompanying package redesign is more complex than an ordinary face-lift.

PLAN FOR THE FUTURE

Many times, packaging designers who tackle a change-of-focus project are planning for products that aren't yet in place—or even those that haven't been conceptualized yet. Often, a company is gearing up to extend an existing brand into a variety of different flavors, strengths, or specialties, or plans to add different kinds of product to forward the brand into different categories.

The design architecture you create now will carry the company into this new era. Work closely with your client to examine the company's business plan, including future plans for growth and expansion and predictions for market change. Forward thinking can ensure the packaging system you design will maintain strong "line logic" down the road.

UNCOVER THE COMPANY'S TRUE NATURE

Over years of arbitrary brand tweaks (frequently overseen by changing regimes of product managers), a brand and its packaging can become muddled. A change in focus is a perfect opportunity to get to the bottom of what the brand is actually all about, and to convey that message through packaging design. A few of the projects in this book exemplify this perfectly, such as the way Pearls Olives discovered the fun and fanciful nostalgia surrounding its product, or how Café de Lya returned to its Mother Earth roots.

AVOID BANDWAGONS

Shunning design fads is good advice, no matter what the reason for redesign, but particularly in the case of a change-of-focus project, thinking in terms of longevity is key. "It's important not to let your package be gimmicky," says Lynn Ritts, creative director for PrimoAngeli:Fitch in San Francisco. "Don't chase the microtrends." After the trendy competitors have come and gone, your solid packaging system, based on strong brand equity, will continue to prevail.

before

after

Rust-Oleum has controlled 75 percent of the aerosol paint market, particularly with its top-branded rust-preventive paint. However, the eighty-year-old company had to diversify to stay competitive as the home-improvement market evolved. The company set out to offer a line of products that focused on specific customer needs while also acting as a product family that could be displayed as a lineup at retail markets to demonstrate how the individual products could be used together.

Rust-Oleum approached creative firm One Zero Charlie with the task of developing a new look for the brand. However, as a company that constantly touts its long heritage (including the fascinating story of its sea captain founder who developed a fish-oil-based paint to prevent rust), Rust-Oleum needed to revisit its past. One Zero Charlie's designers underwent the firm's "brand restoration" process to revitalize the brand and allow it to grow yet remain its stalwart self.

Fruit to Go

DESIGN
Karacters Design Group, Vancouver,
British Columbia, Canada
LEAD DESIGNER
Nancy Wu
ASSOCIATE CREATIVE DIRECTOR
Matthew Clark
CREATIVE DIRECTOR
Maria Kennedy
PROJECT MANAGER
Angela Hartshorne
ACCOUNT DIRECTOR
Brendan Kelly
SENIOR PRODUCER
John Ziros

COMPUTER PRODUCTION
Lisa Good, Peter Hall
ILLUSTRATOR
Adam Rogers
PHOTOGRAPHER
Clinton Hussey
ILLUSTRATED TYPE
Ivan Angelic
PREPRESS
Southern Graphics
PRINTER
Sonoco Flexible Packaging
MARKET
Canada

before

Fruit to Go, a dried-fruit snack, has always been a mother's favorite; the number one fruit snack in Canada was a 100 percent natural alternative to candy and chips. Even the flavors were simple and tame—all variations on the doctor-ordered apple. The packaging reflected this image—attractive and mature looking, the package appealed to parents looking for lunchbox ideas. Kids, who notoriously shun anything their parents appreciate, weren't asking for the snack when their parents shopped, and sales were beginning to slip.

The final packaging is cool enough for kids, respectable enough for moms, and brilliant enough to skate, swim, and jump right into any family's shopping cart.

Fruit to Go Design Process

The manufacturer of these fruit snacks, Sun-Rype, is as wholesome as they come: the 55-year-old company, based in an agricultural corridor of western Canada, specializes in natural fruit juices and fruit snacks. Sun-Rype's Fruit to Go has long been the number one fruit snack, a favorite in Canada among parents looking for healthy snack alternatives.

REASON FOR REDESIGN

Although Fruit to Go still led its category, sales had flattened and begun to decline. Sun-Rype conducted research that showed adults still loved the goodness of the snack and kids still liked the taste, but both parents and kids found the packaging too adult targeted and not something that kids would actually request. Because 80 percent of purchases were for households with children, Sun-Rype realized it needed to encourage kids to ask for the snack from their parents.

The manufacturer decided to expand the line, adding new flavors and a stronger fruit taste. Sun-Rype dropped the base ingredient, apple, from its product descriptions and, instead, promoted the line's flavor variety. The packaging also needed to tap into the key insight that Fruit to Go was considered "healthy fuel for active kids."

REDESIGN OBJECTIVES

- Create a cool, energetic image that would attract kids and preteens
- Communicate to parents that the product was the same healthy, responsible fruit snack as always
- Expand the flavors and varieties offered under the Fruit to Go brand

THE RESULTS

Fruit to Go kept its top spot in the market, and Sun-Rype saw a 25 percent rise in sales from the spring 2003 rollout. Thanks to a national advertising and public-relations campaign aimed at kids combined with a radical on-shelf debut, awareness of the fruit snack brand also rose 14 percent throughout the country.

ACTIVITY FOCUS

1

2–4

5

6

C06 / M80 / Y0 / K0
pms 238 · C90 / M10 / Y0 / K0
pms 306 · C0 / M80 / Y60 / K0
pms 1777 · C0 / M20 / Y80 / K0
pms 1235 · C45 / M65 / Y0 / K0
pms 2577

C0 / M100 / Y40 / K5
pms 205 · C0 / M50 / Y100 / K0
pms 1375 · C0 / M55 / Y15 / K0
pms 190 · C45 / M0 / Y100 / K0
pms 375

7

8

9

1
The manufacturer Sun-Rype turned to Karacters Design Group to help design a new architecture for a planned rollout of an expanded line of flavors. Additionally, Sun-Rype wanted to explore how to appeal to kids ages 6 to 10. They adopted the concept of "healthy fuel for active kids" for the products. Karacters set out to explore all the directions this concept could take them, referring to comic books, video games, skateboards, and other pop culture favorites to avoid the cute or childish approach common among fruit snacks.

2–4
The designer and client narrowed ideas to different directions: "contemporary action," "fruit as fuel," and "activity." Relying on the feedback of focus groups, the team finally decided to combine the ideas of activity with the concept of fruit as energy.

5, 6
After selecting the concept, the next challenge was finding the right illustrations that would serve all those purposes. "We knew we didn't want anything photographic, serious, childish, or too adult," says designer Nancy Wu. And the illustrations couldn't be trendy either—they needed to stand the test of time. Illustrator Adam Rogers experimented with styles before discovering the boldly outlined shapes of skateboarders, snowboarders, soccer players, and other characters that would eventually serve as the background graphics.

7
Karacters convinced the client to move away from its trademark blue as the most prominent color on the wrapper. Therefore, Wu was free to use a vibrant color palette that was cool to kids and conveyed energy. The blue remained as the recognizable element from the previous package, and a consistent green also tied the differently colored packages together.

8
The old Fruit to Go logo was drawn in a bouncy, adult style. Karacters redesigned the logo to speak directly to kids, in a way that didn't pander to them. According to Wu, covers of the early French-edition Tintin comic book covers inspired the new typeface.

9
Karacters turned to a unique color mix to bring out the brightness in the real fruit images while representing the brand color effectively. Previous fruit images were muddy when shot differently and printed at a much smaller size, Wu explains. Instead, perfectly shaped fruit was shot with strong 3-D modeling to look hyperreal.

La Milita

DESIGN
Ideas Frescas, San Salvador, El Salvador
DESIGN AND ART DIRECTION
Ana Gabriela Larios
MARKET
United States and Canada

before

The jar used by a coalition of El Salvadoran honey producers featured a plain label with a friendly illustration of bees and a straightforward name: "Central American honey." The jar was suitable for local distribution, but when the producers launched an initiative to aggressively market the honey in North American markets, they needed something more sophisticated, memorable, and representative of the product's Latin origins.

At first, the client wanted to move to a PET plastic bottle to save costs. Ideas Frescas felt the original glass jar with the copper-colored lid lent more credence to the honey as a high-quality product. Potential buyers reacted the same way, so the glass remained, complete with new labels on the bottle and lid. The new La Milita is at once elegant, fun, and memorable—and its origins are easy to recognize.

La Milita Design Process

Beekeeping for the production of natural honey is a big business in El Salvador, and over the years, the country's sticky sweet product has earned a reputation for purity, freshness, and quality. A trade association called VACE (an initialism that is also referred to in English as the Beekeeping Cluster) has for the past twenty years promoted the export of the honey overseas. In the past few years, however, the El Salvadoran government has recognized honey as one of the many agricultural products that have potential in the U.S. and Canadian markets. With the passage of the Central American Free Trade Agreement on the horizon, there has been an increased push to market El Salvadoran honey in North America.

REASON FOR REDESIGN
The Beekeeping Cluster commissioned a new design for its honey jars to appeal to a wide range of American and Canadian consumers and also to communicate the origin and quality of the product inside. The package in which the honey was originally sold featured a cute illustration of two bees on a white label that covered a clear glass jar. But the exporters needed to convey more immediately an image that was modern, memorable, and unmistakably Latin.

REDESIGN OBJECTIVES
- Create a package that reflects the unique propositions of Central American honey: pure, natural, fresh, and high quality
- Design a memorable and innovative honey jar that is original and modern, yet friendly and appealing
- Fill an existing gap in the U.S. and Canadian honey markets with Central American honey and clearly communicate an authentic Latin flair

THE RESULTS
The package has been very well received by potential U.S. and Canadian buyers, with whom the exporters are still in negotiations. The El Salvadoran government has expressed its faith in the potential success of the product and has backed it with a $20,000 subsidy—a major part of the exporters' overall $26,000 budget—to support the promotion of the brand.

1

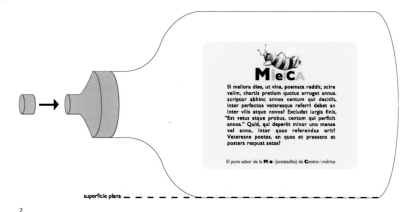

2

3

4

5

6

1
The Beekeeping Cluster hired Ideas Frescas to rebrand the honey and find a successful packaging design to help it accomplish its goals. Ideas Frescas explored a couple of different routes. One idea was to brand the honey MIELCA (an initialism for Miel de Centro America, or Central American honey) and to portray the friendliness and fresh-ness of the brand. For this direction, the firm's illustrator created whimsical bee characters to represent the product.

2
This direction involved a structural redesign that was as original as the package's label. However, the client worried that the overall impression didn't communicate the honey's origins—a major objective of the project.

3–5
The other route Ideas Frescas explored was La Milita, a more exotic brand that was distinctly Latin. Designer Ana Gabriela Larios sketched a wide-eyed Latin beauty startled by a bee's elaborate flight pattern. The direction was fun and presented an immediately recognizable Latin American flavor. This is the brand that the client ultimately selected.

6
La Milita's new logo—a cheerful, bubbly script drawn from glistening honey—presents a friendly, organic image for the product.

Live a Little

DESIGN
Ingalls & Associates, San Francisco, California
MARKET
United States

before

Live a Little, a gourmet line of salad dressings by a little company in the San Francisco Bay Area, had developed a small, but loyal, following through its sales in the refrigerated sections of specialty groceries. But as the company expanded, the plastic tub Live a Little used to package its tasty dressings wasn't helping it convey the upscale image that justified its price and standing in high-end food stores.

The redesigned label was applied to a slender glass bottle that allows the contents to show through. The lively, quirky graphics, combined with healthy white space and unexpected layout choices, capture the attention of gourmet food lovers.

Live A Little
GOURMET FOODS®

VERY BLUE CHEESE
DRESSING

9 FLUID OZ. (266 ML)
KEEP REFRIGERATED

Live a Little Design Process

This little homegrown, gourmet salad dressing company is the brainchild of professional chef Virginia Davis, who had worked as an executive chef and pastry chef at numerous prestigious restaurants throughout the San Francisco Bay Area. With Live a Little, Davis set out to create a line of fresh salad dressings. Traditional varieties such as Very Blue Cheese and Bold Balsamic Vinaigrette gave consumers what they wanted—their old favorites, with full flavor and natural ingredients.

REASON FOR REDESIGN

Already in business for a couple of years, Live a Little had developed a comfortable following, selling its dressings in plastic tubs in specialty food stores in California and elsewhere. But the company was growing and expanding into Whole Foods and other major natural-food stores, and it needed an image more upscale than a plastic tub could deliver. So Live a Little turned to Ingalls & Associates to explore new packaging design to help the dressings shine in the refrigerated section of shops and supermarkets.

REDESIGN OBJECTIVES

- Switch to a glass jar as the new container for Live a Little salad dressings, and design a label that would be resilient to the jars' oily contents
- Strike a balance between providing a new, more upscale design, which would allow the dressings to succeed in larger retail environments, and retaining enough brand equity to speak to the dressings' loyal followers
- Design a palette of colors flexible and expandable enough to suit a growing number of varieties

THE RESULTS

The perception of the product since the new packaging launch has been very good, says Ingalls & Associates principal Tom Ingalls. Buyers at the retail stores where the product is sold feel more confident that the product will sell at its price point now that it has achieved a more gourmet look.

I've learned from years as a professional chef that fine cooking is as much about managing time as managing flavor. Great chefs prepare whatever they can, as far in advance as possible, without compromising quality. Adhering to these same standards, *Live A Little Gourmet Foods* offers you the finest ingredients, years of experience, and a little extra time. Try some of my favorite foods exactly as I serve them in my own home.

Virginia David
Chef, Owner

PO Box 10916, Oakland California 94610
888.744.2300 info@livealittle.com
www.livealittle.com

LIVE A LITTLE
GOURMET FOODS®

MANGO LIME
DRESSING

NET WEIGHT 10OZ. (280G)

Ingredients: expeller pressed canola oil, sherry vinegar, mango puree, sugar, fresh shallots, fresh scallions, lime juice from concentrate, salt, natural mango flavor, black pepper, xanthan gum.

Mango Lime: An exotic blend of sweet and tangy flavors. Great for summer salads with berries and nuts; complements butter lettuce or spinach. An ideal sauce for grilled fish or drizzled on fruit salads.

NUTRITION FACTS

0 27724 43750 9

1

2

3

4

5

 →

6

1
The owner of Live a Little was particularly concerned about alienating her already loyal customers. Ingalls & Associates began exploring possible designs, looking for ways to subtly add elements from the original packaging while using more natural, upscale colors and graphics. In this comp, for example, the checkered bar is reinvented to be much less prominent and uses shades of brown rather than black and white.

2–4
In these comps, the checkered pattern is used in various ways. The designers also picked up and exaggerated the hat from the dancing chef motif on the original packaging. The three comps show different treatments, from colorfully saturated to clean and simple.

5
In the end, however, Live a Little's owner made the business decision to stick a little more closely to her brand equities. Ingalls expanded on the existing color palettes, kept the black-and-white checkerboard, and retained the typeface from the original. But the designers organized the elements in a way to better use space and make the labels more unique. The designers researched and developed a color palette to characterize each flavor.

6
The dancing chef, originally squeezed into the logo, now became a small, but prominent design motif.

Origin

DESIGN
Wink, Minneapolis, Minnesota
CREATIVE DIRECTORS
Richard Boynton and Scott Thares
DESIGNERS
Richard Boynton, Scott Thares, and Dawn Selg

MARKET
United States

before

The former packaging for Target stores' Origin dietary supplements, true to retail private-label standards, was purposefully generic—no images, special branded type treatments, or other graphical treatments intended to create a unique image for the products. Instead, the plain bottles were meant to appear as the low-cost equivalent to better-known national brands.

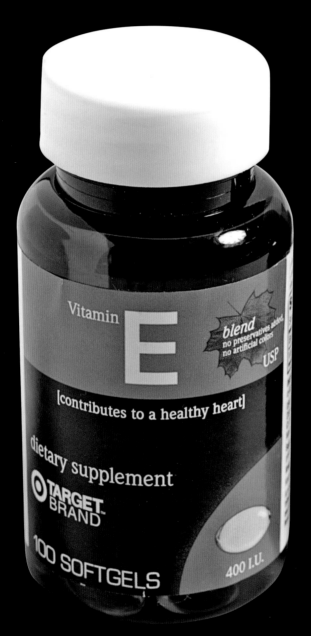

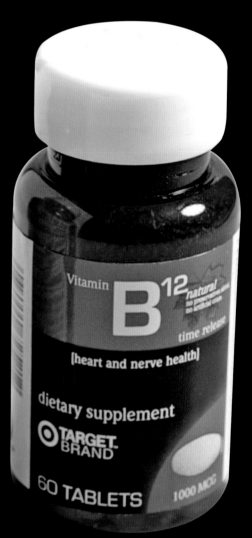

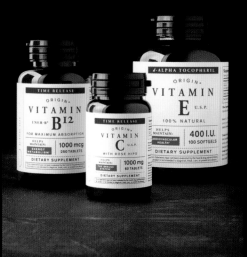

The redesigned labels combine an antique, apothecary look with a touch of modernity, giving the products a natural, high-end look. The products' sales have benefited from the gorgeous new packaging, leveling the playing field between Target's private label and the national brands.

Origin Design Process

Target Corp., like many other major chain retailers, offers a number of private-label products alongside national brands for price-conscious consumers. One of these product lines is a dietary supplement offering—vitamins, minerals, and herbal remedies with the same ingredients as national-brand supplements. True to typical private-label treatments, the original bottles for the Target dietary supplements were purposefully plain, immediately suggesting a generic alternative to the trademarked designs of competitors' bottles.

REASON FOR REDESIGN

Company-wide, however, Target began to move more toward unique designs for its private brands. Products in the Target pharmacy were also moving in a new direction: the stores were beginning to specialize in a more natural and holistic approach to health with their private-label pharmaceutical products. The Target vitamins and nutritional supplements needed to fall in line with this rebranding, which required a new name and new packaging design.

REDESIGN OBJECTIVES

- Create packaging that would reflect the selected name and direction for Target's rebranded private-label nutritional supplements
- Develop a design that would clearly communicate product information and create an easy, recognizable organizational structure for the many different kinds of product
- Adhere to the Target pharmacy's new, holistic approach toward healthcare

THE RESULTS

Target has raved over the sales of the new Origin line, telling creative firm Wink that they're selling much better than the company ever expected. "I went into a Target to see how they were displayed the first week they were released and was treated to seeing a late-thirties mom (the primary target market) shopping for her dietary supplements," says Richard Boynton, the creative director for the project. "She picked up the Origin bottle and a competitor's bottle, compared the two—which obviously have the same ingredients—and then put the Origin bottle in her cart, along with three other supplements from the same line!"

1

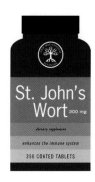

Vitamin C
500 mg

dietary supplement

enhances the immune system

100 TABLETS

Zinc
600 mg

dietary supplement

enhances the immune system

500 TABLETS

St. John's
Wort 300 mg

dietary supplement

enhances the immune system

350 COATED TABLETS

2

ORIGIN · STANDARDIZED · Dietary Supplement

1000 mg

Vitamin
C
with Rose Hips

Enhances the Immune System

100 TABLETS

ORIGIN · STANDARDIZED · Dietary Supplement

1000 mg

Zinc

Enhances the Immune System

100 TABLETS

ORIGIN · STANDARDIZED · Dietary Supplement

1000 mg

St. John's
Wort

Enhances the Immune System

100 TABLETS

3

1
Wink also started exploring package designs for the potential identities. For the name Millennium, designers experimented with modern-feeling aluminum cylindrical tins as well as glass bottles and colorful graphics.

2
Designs for the New Millennium approach were more natural feeling, with a leafy tree logo and earthy colors to convey the all-natural ingredients of the products. Shaded stripes on each bottle contained the many necessary layers of product information.

3
Designers also explored the potential name Origin, going down the path of a simple, clean, graphical structure with meaningful touches of color.

4
When Target decided to rebrand its pharmacies, the chain engaged Wink to create a new design for the extensive line of vitamins and minerals. However, Target was still weighing a number of different names and identities for its pharmacies as a whole, as well for as the supplements. Wink began developing logo ideas for all of the potential names and approaches.

5, 6
Target ultimately rebranded its pharmacies to focus on a more holistic and organic approach and selected the Origin name for the supplements line. Wink's designers altered their focus on a simple graphic design with little ornamentation but a great deal of character, allowing for straightforward organization of product information on the label but building a strong image using type and hints of rich colors.

4

WHOLE HERB EXTRACT

ORIGIN™

ST. JOHN'S
WORT U.S.P.

NATURAL DIETARY SUPPLEMENT

ENHANCES
the imune system

IMPROVES
mental acuity

400 mg
100 TABLETS

EASY TO SWALLOW COATED CAPLETS

This statement has not been evaluated by the food & drug administration.
This product is not intended to diagnose, treat, cure, or prevent any disease.

ACTUAL SIZE

400
mcg

This statement has not been evaluated by the food & drug administration. This product is not intended to diagnose, treat, cure, or prevent any disease.

5

6

Black Pearls Olives had been on the market since 1992 and were a hit with consumers. So when the manufacturer Musco Olive Products Inc. acquired its largest competitor, adding lines of green and specialty olives, they wanted to build a new packaging architecture to accommodate all the new varieties while reinforcing the well-known Pearls brand. Research showed that consumers recognized the yellow color and bursting olives on the old label design. Additionally, the name "Black Pearls" was widely recognized and liked. Tesser concluded that an effective redesign would feature these key elements prominently— while improving on the rest.

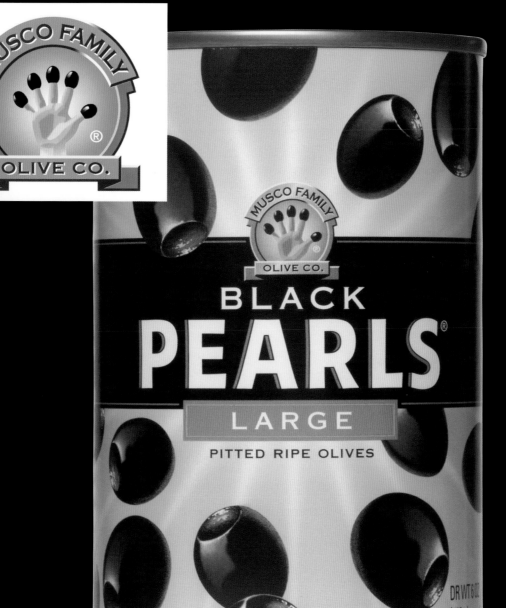

The label redesign presented an opportunity to rebrand the parent company itself. Research proved that customers knew the Black Pearls name, but had no awareness of Musco Olive Products. In fact, many thought Musco sounded like a big corporate conglomerate. It was time to get credit for the fact that Musco was a family-run business and develop a memorable mark that consumers could relate to and connect with.

Pearls Olives Design Process

Since 1940, the family-owned-and-operated Musco Olive Products in northern California packaged olives for the food-service industry, and in the past decade hit the retail market with its Black Pearls line of black olives. But since purchasing its largest competitor in 1999, the company has branched out with green and specialty olives—and has become the first company to offer a complete line of retail olives at all price points.

1

REASON FOR REDESIGN

Because it no longer focused exclusively on black olives, Musco needed a brand identity that more accurately summed up its quality and breadth. Market research showed that the Pearls name stood out in consumers' minds, while the manufacturer identity barely made the charts. The company decided to rebrand itself and its olives and wanted a system of packaging that would distinguish the subbrands (Green, Black, Mediterranean) at first glance on the store shelf.

Additionally, Musco and its creative firm, Tesser Inc., agreed that olives as a food were due for a rebrand. "Traditionally, olive branding approaches had ranged from 'utilitarian foodstuff' and 'mamma-mia Italian ingredient' for black olives to 'fancy-schmancy appetizer' for specialty olives," says Tré Musco, CEO and creative director of Tesser (who, as a member of the Musco family himself, understood the client's needs all too well). "American consumers, however, have long used olives as a convivial snack item for get-togethers. The creative team felt strongly it was time to give olives credit for being the healthy, versatile, and family-friendly snack item that they are."

REDESIGN OBJECTIVES

- Retain key brand elements such as the Pearls name, color yellow, and "bursting" olives
- Update the parent company brand and integrate new product offerings
- Complement a widespread marketing campaign

THE RESULTS

The new Pearls line is proving to be a major retail success, with penetration into 70% of the U.S. market, and volume sales that rank it first in its category. The manufacturer reports that brand recognition is at an all-time high. Additionally, consumers have been writing to Musco to report their delight with the label design and its effect on their purchasing decisions.

2

3

5

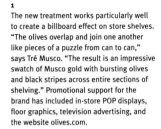

4

6

7

1
The new treatment works particularly well to create a billboard effect on store shelves. "The olives overlap and join one another like pieces of a puzzle from can to can," says Tré Musco. "The result is an impressive swatch of Musco gold with bursting olives and black stripes across entire sections of shelving." Promotional support for the brand has included in-store POP displays, floor graphics, television advertising, and the website olives.com.

2
With Tesser's help, the company was renamed Musco Family Olive Co. New identity explorations included rustic scenes of olive harvests and romantic Italian landscapes.

3, 4
Ultimately, the team decided that the olive category itself was due for a rebrand, and opted for a nontraditional approach. For years, Tesser had used a child's hand with olive-capped fingers in Musco's promotional materials. Initially, translating this image into a corporate mark seemed like it would be difficult. Early sketches looked cartoonish and odd.

5
Finally, Tesser hit upon the idea of rendering the hand in the style of 1930s and 1940s Streamline-era illustration. "Once we figured out the Streamline style, it all fell into place," says Tré Musco, CEO and creative director. "We hired Laura Smith to create the illustration, and I think she did a great job of making the hand fun and approachable, yet serious enough to represent a sixty-year-old company." The creative team created a frame and type treatment for the mark, and the Musco Seal was born. The seal is used by itself on retail packaging, and is combined with the Musco logotype on corporate materials.

6
In addition to the Musco Seal, the final label designs feature a black belly band, with the new Pearls logotype and variety descriptor. Olive sizes are called out in colored bars below the band. Green and Kalamata varieties come in jars, so the labels feature only the golden burst (without olives). Sliced and chopped olives have their own "bursting olive" illustrations, showing customers exactly what they're purchasing.

7
The new Pearls line uses descriptors to distinguish the products from one another, while the design combines a richer, proprietary gold color and hyperrealistic bursting olives with the rebranded Musco hand seal to give the product a sense of energy and fun.

Extreme Makeovers:
LEAVE BEHIND INEFFECTIVE DESIGN

Beefeater Crown Jewel

DESIGN
Fitch, London, United Kingdom
MARKET
Worldwide

The old bottle for Crown Jewel, Beefeater's premium gin, created a cool, precious image for the brand, but the colorless bottle and its offbeat shape put Crown Jewel at a disadvantage in the crowded, cost-conscious, duty-free space.

In the gin category, other brands have "owned" colors (including Bombay Sapphire's blue and Tanqueray's green). In this tradition, and to make the bottle memorable, Fitch selected a rich purple glass for the bottle. The color is regal and jewellike, combined with a bottle cut asdistinctively as a gemstone. Topped with a gold-colored cap, the overall effect lives up to the product's name.

Beefeater Crown Jewel
Design Process

Beefeater, a stalwart brand of gin for nearly two centuries, prides itself on its heritage and quality—it's the only producer that distills its gin in England, where gin originated in the seventeenth century. Beefeater's staple brand, London Dry, is consistently rated at the top of its class.

But for true gin lovers, Beefeater offers its premium version, Crown Jewel, a berry-and-citrus-infused gin with a smoother finish. Backed by the heralded Beefeater brand, the premium gin was beginning to make its entrance into duty-free markets in the United Kingdom and around the world.

REASON FOR REDESIGN

As Beefeater geared up to promote Crown Jewel, the company realized the bottle's look didn't support its desired top-of-the-line image—or the price that went with it. The bottle looked nothing like London Dry, the parent brand, nor did it at all resemble other gins on the shelf, shrinking in its squat bottle beside its tall, thick competitors. The colorless bottle, while giving the bottle a pure, platinum look, rendered the gin practically invisible next to more colorful brands.

REDESIGN OBJECTIVES

- Promote Crown Jewel as an ultrapremium brand in the Beefeater family
- Appeal to the primarily male audience and support the brand's bold, adventurous image
- Increase sales and distribution of Crown Jewel in the duty-free market worldwide

THE RESULTS

At press time, the launch was too recent to gather real financial results. However, at Crown Jewel's relaunch during the October 2003 Cannes Duty-Free Fair, the trade positively received the new bottle and the product within it.

ABCDEFGHIJKLMNOP

QRSTUVWXYZ?!

1

2

3

4

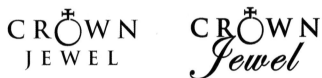

5

6

7

1
At the beginning of the project, creative firm Fitch:London looked at every possible direction for the bottle design. The designers looked into all aspects of Crown Jewel and Beefeater's heritage and brand name. Beefeater, named for the guards who watch over the Tower of London and the royal crown jewels housed safely inside the tower, provided initial inspiration for sketches and design directions.

2–4
After more in-depth research, the designers considered a number of different ideas. From the history of the Tower of London emerged the tradition of the ravens, pitch-black birds who guard the British crown jewels. One design concept involved representing the raven theme—symbolizing masculinity, self-assuredness, and intelligence—on the Crown Jewel bottle.

5
Other concepts focused on the heritage of the gin, calling on images of the St. George's Cross (an old English emblem) as a reminder of its British origins and on crests and Old English type to suggest the product's long history.

6, 7
The raven concept won the contest. The designers and the client also identified a number of other elements that had to be represented: the orb (part of the collection of Crown Jewels); the Beefeater guards, also known as Yeoman Warders, who guard the ravens and the jewels; and the prestigious International Wine and Spirits Competition awards the gin has won. The designers found ways to combine these elements smoothly into the design, including making the orb the *O* in the logo, with the raven swooping down to protect it.

Canyon Road

DESIGN
MOD/Michael Osborne Design, San Francisco, California
MARKET
United States and Europe

before

The old Canyon Road packaging was suffering on the shelf alongside newcomers and splashier labels designed to grab the attention of bang-for-the-buck consumers.

The attractive, artistic new bottle is a big hit with consumers and retailers alike.

Canyon Road Design Process

Based in the Alexander Valley of Sonoma, California, Canyon Road produces wines that have "casual sophistication"—they're easy to drink and affordable to buy. In fact, the wines occupy one of the most cutthroat store shelves—the $5.99 to $6.99 California blends—where packaging design and name are the only things that give a wine a chance.

The wines had a strong presence in Europe, where they were marketed as traditional California wine. In the United States, however, the brand was "gathering dust on the bottom shelf at retail," according to creative firm Michael Osborne Design. This situation was especially true in the current state of the wine industry. Grape reserves were swelling as demand dropped off, farmers overproduced, and prices plummeted—factors that added to the competition in lower-priced categories.

1

2

REASON FOR REDESIGN

Sales were flat, and the unremarkable label design was not helping. Canyon Road was ready to shed its traditional coats and do something revolutionary to jump-start sales. Research showed that Canyon Road's most valuable brand equity was its name, not the bottle or label design. Therefore, the company and its creative firm decided to try a drastic overhaul of the wine's image.

REDESIGN OBJECTIVES

- Drastically change the look of Canyon Road wines to create a memorable brand image
- Capitalize on Canyon Road's existing equity by emphasizing the brand name
- Appeal to American consumers with a cutting-edge design that would turn heads

THE RESULTS

Sales are soaring in both the United States and Europe. In some cases, retailers have actually moved the wine up a shelf or two, and the brand possesses extraordinary shelf presence with its savvy Arts and Crafts look.

3

4

5

6

7

8

1, 2
With an anything-goes attitude, Canyon Road and Michael Osborne Design jumped into the redesign process, exploring every possible approach in early sketches. They adhered to a loose set of guidelines in attempting to capture the spirit of California with a fun, casual, and elegant style.

3
The client and creatives agreed that Canyon Road's singular brand equity was its name, so early design ideas played off of that with the attempt to work angular canyon cliffs into the label.

4, 5
Early approaches involved everything from a subtle approach using muted and distinguished colors to attempts to make the label jovial and artistic. The bottle on the left (4) was one of the first approaches, which later evolved into the final approach, that emphasized the *C* from the product name
in the design.

6, 7
After the designers struck on the idea of using the block letter *C* as the foundation for the design with an Arts and Crafts typeface for the name, the client and creatives fine-tuned the details, such as what the neckband would look like and where vintage and other product information would reside.

8
The final labels used subdued jewel colors to classify the different varieties of wine.

Fairytale Brownies

DESIGN
Lee Design Studio, Encino, California

ART DIRECTORS
**David Kravetz, Fairytale Brownies, and
Elisabeth Spitalny Lee, Lee Design Studio**

DESIGNERS
Elisabeth Spitalny Lee and Tesia Rynkiewicz

MARKET
United States

before

Fairytale's beverage packaging was uninspired. Small silver and purple labels crammed product information into rectangular text boxes. The whimsical elf logo was barely visible, and it was difficult to tell the coffee, cocoa, and tea packages apart.

The goal was to make the different products' bags complement each other while still looking completely distinct. They also needed to share colors on press. The unique redesign transformed the overall brand offering.

Fairytale Brownies Design Process

Fairytale Brownies Inc., the dream of two childhood best friends, Eileen Spitalny and David Kravetz, was attracting a good deal of attention for its gourmet Belgian chocolate brownies and accompanying line of coffee and cocoa in its hometown of Chandler, Arizona. After a number of media mentions, including magazine articles and a profile on cable TV's Food Network, Fairytale began to attract the attention of food lovers across the country, and its mail-order and ecommerce services branched out.

REASON FOR REDESIGN

Fairytale approached Elisabeth Lee of Lee Design Studios to rethink the company's packaging template. A great deal of product information was crammed onto a tiny label, which was applied to a clear polypropylene wrapper around the individual brownies. The same went for the beverages: crowded labels crammed a list of ingredients and branding imagery into a tiny space, which swam on their brown paper bags. The contents were delectable, but the company's branding was getting lost in its own packaging.

In addition to the need for a redesign, Fairytale also needed to keep their products fresh longer, especially now that they were beginning to ship products around the world. This would require a rethinking of materials and printing processes as well.

REDESIGN OBJECTIVES

- Reinforce the whimsical "fairytale" brand image, giving more play to the company's jaunty elfin logo
- Create more real estate on the labels and coffee/cocoa bags to provide room for more information such as nutritional analysis, ingredients, and a UPC bar code
- Develop tamper-resistant packaging and improve the freshness seal for the beverages; replace the polypropylene wrapper with a barrier film to give the brownie a longer shelf life; and create a faster, more accurate wrapping and labeling process for the individually wrapped brownies

THE RESULTS

Cofounder David Kravetz says the new packaging gives the products a premium look. For a boutique brownie business, that's essential, Kravetz says, because more than 95 percent of the products Fairytale Brownies sells are gifts. Now that the beverages sport their shiny, swirly packaging, Fairytale promotes them as stand-alone gifts, rather than being part of a gift set—proof that their dreamy, revamped look makes them exceptional gifts by themselves.

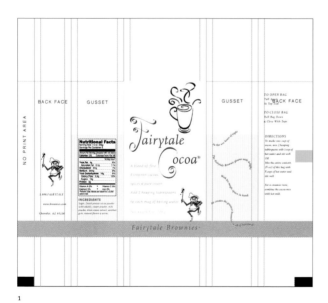

1

2

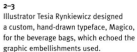

3

INGREDIENTS:
Sugar, butter, unsweetened Belgian chocolate, eggs, flour (wheat flour, niacin, iron, thiamin mononitrate, riboflavin, folic acid), baking powder (baking soda, cornstarch, sodium aluminum sulfate, monocalcium phosphate). Chandler, Arizona 85226

6 06961 00001 3

WHEN MICROWAVING, REMOVE WRAPPER & USE LOW POWER

NUTRITION FACTS:
Serving size: 1/2 brownie (42g), Servings 2, Amount Per Serving: **Calories** 198, Fat Cal. 105, **Total Fat** 12g (18% DV), Sat. Fat 7g (35% DV), **Cholest.** 55g (19% DV), **Sodium** 108mg (5% DV), **Total Carb.** 22g (7% DV), Fiber 2g (5% DV), Sugars 19g, **Protein** 2g, Vitamin A (7% DV), Vitamin C (0% DV), Calcium (2% DV), Iron (5% DV). Percent Daily Values (DV) are based on a 2,000 calorie diet.
REFRIGERATE OR FREEZE FOR FRESHNESS

5

4

1
Lee's early design goals, to give the information on the packaging more breathing room and really celebrate the personality of the brand, are clearly evident in this early comp.

2–3
Illustrator Tesia Rynkiewicz designed a custom, hand-drawn typeface, Magico, for the beverage bags, which echoed the graphic embellishments used.

4
At this point, the designer encountered a glitch: printing restrictions when using the flexo printing process required Lee to use a minimum-stroke keyline around the artwork. Lee was forced to rethink the company's beloved leaping elf. The result: a unique, recognizable, and practical label for these treasured handmade treats.

5
As its mail-order business grew, Fairytale Brownies needed a more efficient and consistent way to label its products. At the same time, its tiny product labels were crammed with product information that kept its signature logo and colors from standing out. Along with a design overhaul, the company studied the use of "print registration," in which the printer relies on an eyemark printed on the film to center the logo at high printing speeds.

Collaborating with Alcan Packaging in Northbrook, Illinois, Lee and the company investigated a number of printing options before finally choosing an in-line printing process using ULTRASTAR silver metallic ink, which gave the labels a shiny, foil-like look. Lee developed a template for the new packaging using the signature silver color.

Frutier

DESIGN
Cincodemayo Design Studio, Monterrey,
Nuevo Leon, Mexico
DESIGN AND ART DIRECTION
Mauricio Alanis, Cincodemayo Design Studio

ILLUSTRATION
Jesus Aberto, Cincodemayo Design Studio
DESIGN COLLABORATION
Emilio Cruz, Embotelladoras Arca
MARKET
Northern and Central Mexico

before

Frutier is a Mexican carbonated fruit drink aimed at kids, though you wouldn't have known it from the somber, mature-looking black labels, straightforward photos of fruit, and stiff block logo. Although a poorly rendered, old-fashioned illustration of cartoon cats attempted to correct the image created by the label, it only contributed to the overall awkwardness of the packaging. In addition, the paper label gave the graphics a flat dullness and also peeled off in the moist atmosphere of consumers' refrigerators.

The team chose a plastic label and glossy
print process for the final labels to allow the
energetic graphics to burst from the bottle
while protecting the label against moisture.

Frutier Design Process

Embotelladoras Arca, a giant beverage producer and distributor in northern Mexico, specializes in bottling internationally branded soft drinks such as Coca-Cola and Fanta. It also fosters a number of regionally marketed proprietary brands. Frutier, a carbonated fruit drink, is one of these. Available in four flavors, the juice has been on the market for nearly five years.

REASON FOR REDESIGN

The juice's plastic bottles suffered from outdated graphics and poor print quality. Focus groups frowned on the brand, responding that they didn't identify with the image the fruit juice portrayed. Additionally, the black labels with old, overly literal photographs of fruit didn't mean a thing to the demographic that actually drank the juice—young children. In an attempt to reach out to youngsters, the old label featured a family of cartoon cats, but they were poorly drawn and darkly printed in a corner of the label, almost as an afterthought.

To help this stalwart brand survive in the ultracompetitive beverage industry, the manufacturer consulted with Cincodemayo Design Studio in Monterrey to rethink the label's approach. The creative firm and the manufacturer agreed the packaging needed to serve as the driving force behind the firm's reinvention, so they explored a logo redesign and new illustrations of the cat characters.

REDESIGN OBJECTIVES

- Give the package a colorful, fresh, dynamic look that would help it stand out among its competitors
- Attract the attention of the target demographic—children
- Improve the printing process to do justice to the improved graphics

THE RESULTS

The manufacturer stood behind Cincodemayo's new design with a complete promotional campaign, including point-of-purchase, television, and print ads, as well as new fleet graphics for the delivery trucks. In the six months following the packaging relaunch, sales of the beverage have doubled, according to manufacturer reports.

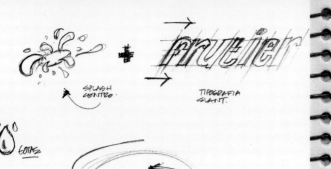

3

4

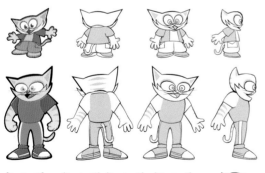

2

5

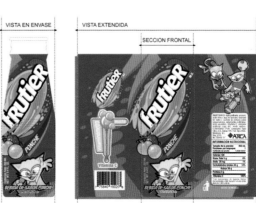

6

7

1

Cincodemayo Design Studio and the manufacturer agreed the label needed to reach out to its target demographic—children—with a more vibrant logo and exciting characters that would intrigue energetic kids. Cincodemayo designers experimented with creating motion on the packaging in initial sketches.

2–4

Cincodemayo played with a number of logo concepts, all incorporating the bright colors of fruit flavors into the various elements. Some initial concepts retained the teardrop that originally topped the logos. Other ideas went to extremes with the concept of cheery fun.

5

Cincodemayo created a cast of cat characters for various uses on the packaging and in advertising. Features of the new characters resembled the look of popular video game and contemporary cartoon characters. In addition, the new "family" now included a female cat to appeal to girls. Active and playful, the cats would eventually drink the beverage, play sports, and jump around on the bottles, so the illustrator needed to determine what the cats would look like from every angle before rendering these action poses.

6

The final logo incorporates the original intent of a liquid splash while working in a rush of movement and color.

7

The designers created new labels that covered the entire bottle instead of wrapping only around the top. Bright colors, cartoonish illustrations, and bubbly type convey product information with energy and youthfulness, in line with the logo and mascots.

Secrets of Success

LEAVE BEHIND INEFFECTIVE DESIGN

When a packaging design is ineffective, the packaging is holding a product back from achieving great things. The quality of the product might be out of this world, but the packaging is simply not doing it justice, or its shelf presence might not be backing up the success of advertising efforts. Therefore, the product should be snatched up in overseas markets or placed on the high-end shelf in the stores, but something is making it fall flat.

CONSIDER NOTHING SACRED

Unlike with outdated designs, in many cases, clients have nothing—or at least little—to lose by taking a risk. Chances are, if the client is seeking a redesign based on an ineffective current packaging, sales are probably less than stellar and the product is likely a shrinking violet on the shelf. Everything is up for consideration: the colors, the typeface, the logo, the illustrations. Whereas clients who are conducting mere refreshes or evolutionary redesigns are protective of their main brand equities, often clients whose packaging is flat-out bombing can be convinced to venture a little further out on the scale with a dramatic redesign.

TURN HEADS

Similarly, although clients who are refreshing outdated packaging are typically gun-shy about making too big of a splash (to avoid alienating loyal consumers or making them nervous about the product's continuity), ineffective designs often require a different approach. In many cases, companies want to take the retail world by storm—because for the first time in a long while, it means that somebody is talking about their product.

"People remember it," says Dennis Whalen of Michael Osborne Design, the firm that redesigned the under-six-dollar wine Canyon Road with a radically unique label. "The label got a 30 percent bump in sales last year. It won't last twenty or thirty years on the market, but that's not the point."

SPELL IT OUT

Sometimes the reason a package design is ineffective is that people just don't get it—either the graphics are misleading or they trigger an inaccurate association in the consumer. This advertising miss can mean certain death for a product, especially when in some retail categories as much as 80 percent of the buying decision is made at the shelf.

before

after

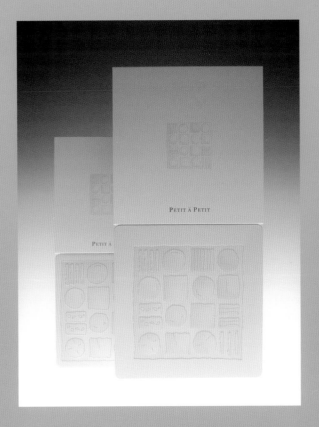

Henri Charpentier is a tony chain of patisseries in Japan. The shops sell miniature works of pastry art, popular among urban gift givers and hosts. The patisseries combine the classic elegance of French pastry with painstaking Japanese aesthetics. The company worried that quality of the packages in which it sold its edible art didn't measure up to the caliber of the products themselves. Boxes came in many different colors, typically printed with whimsical illustrations. Creative firm Curiosity, Inc., also considered that Japanese society places considerable weight on the way products are packaged, taking great pride in handmade wrappings, especially for business gifts. The designers created unique packaging with an austere, modern look that was still fun, with its interesting shapes and textures, to appeal to all consumers.

Nando's Salad Dressings

DESIGN
Cross Colours, Johannesburg, South Africa
MARKET
South Africa and the United Kingdom

before

Nando's has been known worldwide, especially in Great Britain and South Africa, for its peri-peri sauces, popular with lovers of its Portuguese-style chicken restaurants. However, the other products offered by the company weren't selling as well. Research showed the packaging for Nando's salad dressings (top) too greatly resembled that of its peri-peri sauces (bottom).

The ultimate new design—a contemporary, rectangular bottle with light-colored graphics and labels—lets the natural beauty of the dressings shine through with an organic appeal. Retailers and consumers alike sat up and took notice of the dressings.

Nando's Salad Dressings
Design Process

Nando's is a widely known brand with a heritage as eclectic as its products. The South African company owns chicken restaurants across the United Kingdom that specialize in Portuguese-style chicken in a peri-peri sauce. The popular restaurants have now expanded around the world and so have the bottled sauces that Nando's devotees crave. In addition to the in-demand peri-peri sauces, Nando's also produces lines of marinades, cooking sauces, and salad dressings.

REASON FOR REDESIGN
The Mediterranean-style salad dressings weren't selling as well as the company had wanted. Internal research showed the packaging for the dressings too closely resembled that of the peri-peri sauces, so the company decided these dressings needed their own look and feel that differentiated them from Nando's sauces.

REDESIGN OBJECTIVES
- Better differentiate Nando's salad dressings from the rest of the manufacturer's line of sauces
- Give the salad dressings a more upscale feel while still incorporating its branded down-to-earth look
- Attract consumers with a promise of excellent taste and an aesthetically pleasing look

THE RESULTS
The redesign was hugely successful, especially in the U.K. market, where sales increased by 40 percent following the redesign, according to Cross Colours.

1

2

3

4

5

6

1, 2
The designers at Cross Colours set out to create a new salad dressing bottle that retained Nando's casual, earthy look while positioning the brand as more up-market. In initial sketches, they played with illustrations and symbols on the bottle, all the while noting the need for a clean label and the incorporation of Nando's signature stripes.

3, 4
The designers created folksy graphics, which were imprinted on the bottles, and experimented with using the whole bottle as real estate instead of limiting graphics to the centered label, as on the old package.

5, 6
To further set the salad dressings apart from the better-known sauces, Cross Colours experimented with a number of different bottle shapes and adapted the graphics to fit each. Finding the right bottle shape to meet retailers' expectations was perhaps the designers' biggest challenge.

Sir Laurence Olivier,
The Bible—Audio CD Box Set

CLIENT
Liquid 8 Records
DESIGN
Sussner Design Company, Minneapolis, MN
ART DIRECTOR
Derek Sussner

DESIGNER
Brent Gale
MARKET
United States

before

The old packaging for the box set was dated and unsophisticated, with cartoonish art and garish colors. To attract national distributors, the record company needed a more attractive, classic package design.

The final box set's design presents a professional and classic, yet still contemporary look for a beloved product, appealing to distributors, such as BMG, who had previously rejected the set.

Sir Laurence Olivier,
The Bible—Audio CD Box Set
Design Process

Liquid 8 Records in Minneapolis, a company that specializes in "budget" products such as tribute albums and greatest hits collections, purchased a number of assets from another company several years ago. One of those assets was a six-CD box set featuring Sir Laurence Olivier reading the Old Testament. Liquid 8's plan was to distribute the collection widely through distributors with national scope.

REASON FOR REDESIGN

Several large distributors turned down the collection, on the grounds that it didn't live up to the standards they set for the products they represented. The packaging had a lot to do with the rejection: it didn't convey the sophisticated image that a nationally marketed product commanded.

Another reason for the redesign was the timing. Liquid 8 acquired the product shortly after September 11, 2001, when Bible sales were soaring. Many people, no matter what their heritage or religion, were looking for guidance. Since the box set included readings from only the Old Testament, Liquid 8 saw this as a perfect opportunity to market to not only Christian consumers, but people of Jewish and other faiths as well.

Finally, the manufacturer wanted more flexibility with how it packaged and sold the CDs—they wanted to explore selling them individually as well as part of the box set.

REDESIGN OBJECTIVES

- Invoke the timelessness of the Bible by combining classic design treatments with modern elements
- Create an inclusive design that reaches out to consumers of all faiths
- Design each jewel case so that it could be marketed individually, if necessary

THE RESULTS

Before the redesign, Liquid 8 had been actively courting BMG as a potential distributor. BMG rejected them and the collection. After Liquid 8 launched the new packaging, however, BMG agreed to a relationship with Liquid 8 and picked up the box set as part of its line, based on the new, more sophisticated offering.

1

2

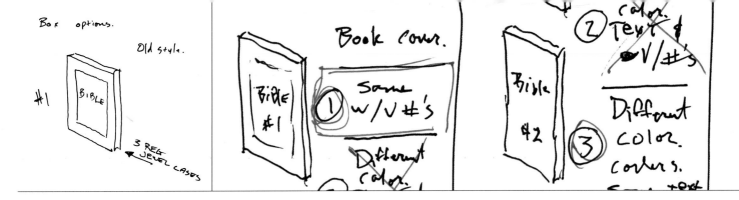

3

4

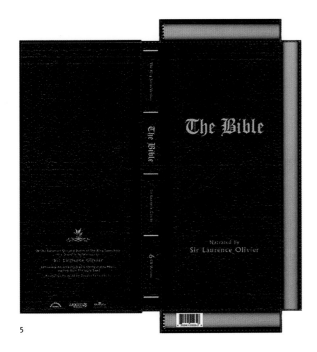

5

6

1, 2
Given that Bible sales were on the rise, Sussner Design Company researched the design elements of the old King James Bible to convey the timelessness of the book. They studied the textures and materials as well as the old etchings and type.

3
Through sketches, the designers at Sussner began sketching possibilities for a box and CD covers that, whether sold together or separately, would evoke images of the classic tome.

4, 5
Original directions adopted the more somber look of old Bibles. The design team mocked up minimalist, black, leather-looking covers. Jumping off from the original direction, the Sussner team gave the elements a more contemporary look. The designers incorporated metallic colors that referenced the foil covers often found on old Bibles. At the same time, they stuck close to familiar, traditional treatments, such as two columns of serif type with decorative initial caps.

6
Each CD had its own theme and look, so the record company could sell them individually. Sussner used elaborate stock illustrations showing Old Testament scenes. Principal Derek Sussner says it was particularly challenging to find the less "morbid" depictions of the sometimes graphic Old Testament stories, so the manufacturer could appeal to the widest range of consumers.

Tend Blends

DESIGN
Hornall Anderson Design Works, Seattle, Washington
MARKET
United States

before

The original bottles used for Tend Blends were simple, with clear labels on clear glass. Although they communicated the natural approach of the bath and beauty products, they appeared homemade and didn't stand out on the shelves. Most important, they failed to communicate a high-end image, which the manufacturer needed to get the products into tony department stores and gift boutiques.

The final packaging system blends an attractive, high-end veneer with a fun, colorful, natural image. Since the relaunch, Tend Blends has increased its popularity in department stores and boutiques.

Tend Blends Design Process

A former beauty editor and gift-boutique owner, Sheena Goldblatt founded Tend Blends as part of a kindergarten project she was working on with her six-year-old son. The company's line of bath and body products are designed for stylish, professional women who have a hard time juggling the three parts of their lives: their careers, their social lives, and their personal time.

The three Tend Blends lines—Work, Rest, and Play—address each, using special flower essences to "release emotional blocks" and help women switch gears seamlessly. The botanic products are each characterized by fun names such as MellowDrama (designed to let "the drama queen abandon her throne"), Creative Juices, and Nap Sugar.

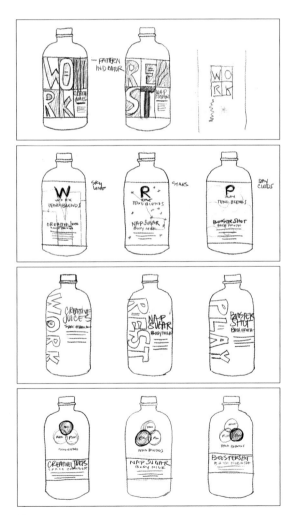

REASON FOR REDESIGN
The company had already broken into high-end department stores such as Barney's and was positioning itself to expand into the high-end gift market. The bottles the company was using were clear, apothecary bottles with plastic tops and clear labels, suggesting a natural, modern approach but not communicating the true story of the product's wholesome blends, chic approach, and carefree attitude.

REDESIGN OBJECTIVES
- Develop a strong shelf presence using unique, memorable packaging graphics
- Create a cohesive design to help position the product for high-end retail channels
- Distinguish between the three lines: Work, Rest, and Play

THE RESULTS
The redesign has successfully invigorated Tend Blends' retail presence at high-end boutiques and department stores. Since the launch, sales have increased and the brand's distribution network has expanded.

1,2

3

4

5

6

7

1, 2
Creative firm Hornall Anderson Design Works began by learning about Tend Blends' vision and personality—which mirrored those of its sassy, fashion-savvy founder. Designers began exploring ways to depict the playful chic of the company and its products.

3
In early comps, designers explored ways to distinguish between the three lines of products (Work, Rest, and Play) while unifying the products as a whole and infusing the brand's dedication to natural lifestyles and stylish fun. In this comp, abstract line drawings embody different lifestyle concepts.

4, 5
Designers also experimented with ways to use the letters of the three different words to vary the lines. In one comp, first letters of the words and their mischievous shadows stand alone, whereas in another, the letters of the four-letter words are stacked like colorful building blocks.

6
Invoking an earthier approach, this comp uses a face reminiscent of tribal masks to depict the emotional needs of the women using the product line.

7
The selected direction uses interlocking circles with the three buzzwords on each bottle—coloring in the featured product line with a color unique to the particular product.

W. M. Barr

DESIGN
Proteus Design, Boston, Massachusetts
MARKET
United States

before

The original packaging for Barr's solvents emphasized the chemical makeup of the product rather than the job for which it was meant to be used. As more DIYers began shopping the category, however, the manufacturer realized the packaging needed to be more user friendly.

Although at first glance the redesigned packages for the three products lines look different from one another, the use of a standard template, a second-level color-coding system, and common images tie the Klean-Strip and Citri-Strip lines together. The packaging for the Klean-Strip thinners line also subtly picks up the same layout as that of the strippers, but it maintains a different look to differentiate between the products' purposes. The careful combination of individuality and continuity make shopping the different lines of products much easier for both the DIYer and professional.

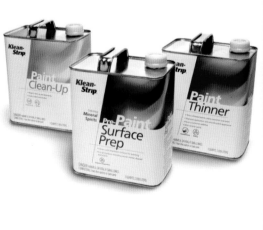

W. M. Barr Design Process

W. M. Barr is a Memphis-based manufacturer that specializes in home-improvement and automotive products—paint thinners, strippers, solvents, and specialty cleaners. The home products in particular comprise a comprehensive line that gives DIYers and professionals all the solutions needed to refinish furniture as well as interior and exterior surfaces.

Barr's products accomplish many different tasks and span two sub-brands, Klean-Strip and Citri-Strip. Because each product has a specific use with its own chemical formula, organizing the product lines was becoming especially complex.

REASON FOR REDESIGN

The previous packaging prominently featured the chemical makeup of each product as the distinguishing factor. However, as the home-improvement consumer changed from the professional contractor to the DIYer and wood-working hobbyist, the product was becoming increasingly harder to shop. The packaging didn't clearly state what each product was for or how to use it, and no visual differentiation existed between the various solvents.

REDESIGN OBJECTIVES

- Create easy-to-understand packaging that emphasizes the solvent's intended job instead of its chemical formula
- Capture the attention of DIY consumers, who in market research exhibited barely any brand loyalty or awareness
- Design packaging lines that are different from one another, making them task oriented

THE RESULTS

The new packaging reached consumers and made the total product line easy to understand, raising the bar for the home-improvement solvents category. The company also used the insight it gained during the thinners and strippers projects to reposition a number of other products, including solvents, which they ultimately redesigned the packaging for as well.

1

2

3

4

5

1–3
Proteus Design explored concepts for paint thinner packages with prominently displayed, descriptive product names and a color classification system.

4, 5
The stripper packages required a slightly different approach—they had to be grouped into family units, so that a color code encompassed several products instead of one.

6
The new logos needed to tie the brands together into a single family of Barr products.

6

Trading Up:
REVAMPING OUTDATED DESIGN

Topo USA
Topo Maps of the Entire USA

Barbie
AVENUE

www.barbie.com

The final new packaging fo
is classy and practical with
sexiness, personifying the
woman consumer.

Avon Design Process

A global company with a universally known brand, Avon is different from many corporate institutions of its caliber simply in the way it has grown: by the dedication and enthusiasm of the millions of women who for decades have sold the products door to door. The company has empowered millions of working women but also has offered housewives a way to easily buy their beauty products from the convenience of their home—a novel concept.

Avon's overall business model is the same today as when it was first conceived in 1886, but the company has evolved with the times to continue to thrive. In the 1990s, Avon saw the need to bring the company into the Internet age, especially as more women consumers were working outside the home. In addition, Avon, which markets its products in more than 140 countries, recognized it could strengthen its brand by moving away from disparate, regionally focused products and toward internationally aligned products and brands. When Andrea Jung, the woman who would eventually take over as CEO, became head of marketing, she consolidated all the lines into large international brands that the company could stand behind.

REASON FOR REDESIGN

As part of this realignment in the late 1990s, Jung ordered a complete package redesign for all of the consolidated brands. Avon was moving into Internet sales, and more than ever, the packaging needed to compete with highbrow designer lines on the market. The company set out to reshape Avon into a world-class beauty brand, so exquisite, modern packaging was an important part of that.

Since its initial redesign, Avon refreshes the brands every three to four years to bring perpetual newness and energy to the customer. The newness concept keeps consumers intrigued and sales representatives excited—two key ingredients for the company's success. "A good deal of the brand's growth comes from redesigns and reformulations," says Kathy Kordowski, vice president of global package development.

REDESIGN OBJECTIVES

- Update and evolve packaging to regularly give sales representatives something new to promote, creating excitement and ultimately increasing sales and market share
- Adhere to global design specifications established for each packaging system, adjusting the specs based on current packaging technology, materials available for each region, and cost
- Consider the needs and input of Avon divisions worldwide to produce a packaging system that will be successful in a variety of cultures and locales

THE RESULTS

"The results to date are very good," says Kordowski. "We have been experiencing strong sales increases globally for the redesigned brands. We feel there is continued opportunity to delight our customers as we continue to update and evolve our packaging."

1

2

1
The company redesigned all of its packaging to consolidate the different brands into a single brand, using only the Avon name and a single logo. In this new design, the Avon Color line broke away from the mold with unexpected angular shapes, a spare type-face, and a metallic blue-black color with platinum accents.

2
To keep things fresh and exciting for sales reps and customers, Avon improved on the Avon Color line in 2004. The in-house packaging design team, choosing to add modern curves back into the mix, created clay models as a framework for the shape and style of the new packaging.

3
The design team then rendered the clean, feminine graphics and added the touches—rounded compact palette trays, hints of metallic, and contemporary all-lowercase type—that complemented the package shapes.

ULTRA COLOR RICH
FULL SIZE LIPSTICK

MY LIP MIRACLE
TRIMLINE LIPCOLOR

NAILWEAR
NAIL ENAMEL

EXTREME
VOLUME
MASCARA

ASTONISHING
LENGTHS
MASCARA

CURLACIOUS
MASCARA

EYESHADOW QUAD COMPACT

EYESHADOW DUO COMPACT

POWDER BLUSH COMPACT

LIQUID
FOUNDATION/BOTTLE

LIQUID
FOUNDATION/TOTTLE

LOOSE FACE POWDER

3

Parham Santana, New York, New York

CREATIVE DIRECTORS
Maruchi Santana and John Parham, Parham Santana

TEAM LEADER/SENIOR ART DIRECTOR
Maryann Mitkowski, Parham Santana

WORLDWIDE GIRLS LICENSING BRAND ...
Cynthia Rapp

MARKET
Worldwide

before

The Barbie packaging hadn't been significantly updated since the 1970s. The bubbly logo and graphics were ...ed and not keeping up with modern fashion, especially compared to ...ndards of design that contemporary girls were used to seeing in clothing and toys.

The feminine, pretty, modern rede[...]
was rolled out for all packaging a[...]
retail fixtures, including bags.

Barbie Design Process

Mattel, the toy manufacturer that makes Barbie, calls its shapely blond sweetheart "the most collectible doll in the world." Since the 1960s, Barbie has done it all, representing just about every career, culture, and celebrity status imaginable. This ambitious doll and her circle of family and friends make up one of the most successful brands in the world. The hot pink color that identifies Barbie doll and accessories boxes is instantly recognizable to most consumers, no matter where the market. Focus groups and studies reveal that in its forty years on the market, Barbie has achieved 100 percent awareness with its target market—three- to twelve-year-old girls and their mothers.

REASON FOR REDESIGN

Barbie's packaging hadn't been redesigned since the 1970s. Although "Barbie pink" was still undeniably powerful with consumers, competitors were beginning to create their own pink packaging to establish an association with the popular brand. Research showed that Mattel's Barbie had established a deeply emotional connection with generations of girls. However, Barbie started her life as a fashion plate—a doll whose clothing, cars, houses, and pursuits reflected the times. As she approached her 40th anniversary, it simply would not do that the Barbie packaging still looked thirty years old. Mattel's branding team, Parham Santana, established a brand statement—"Barbie keeps pace with the times"—around which the millennium-timed redesign was focused.

REDESIGN OBJECTIVES

- Reposition the brand for growth, presenting a contemporary new image and capitalizing on the doll's 40th anniversary
- Define a more consistent and iconic use of the Barbie image and leverage the equity of the Barbie pink
- Reflect girls' intimate relationship with the brand and its characters

THE RESULTS

Retailers and consumers alike adored the new Barbie. "It's the best she's looked in years," one retail buyer said. At FAO Schwarz's flagship store on Fifth Avenue in New York City, the new packaging and merchandising in the new Barbie Experience section alone boosted a double-digit increase in sales.

1

2

3

4

1
In early stages of the redesign, designers explored a series of striped patterns.

2
The final stripe pattern that Mattel selected and tested with focus groups was a pretty, modern motif that reflected the revised goal of the Barbie brand, to keep pace with fashion.

3
The Barbie logo changed from the original bubbly type to a cute, but refined, script designed to appeal to a range of ages and to modern mothers.

4,5
The company rolled out the final packaging for thousands of products in 150 countries and adapted it for point-of-purchase, merchandising, and store fixtures. The international rollout took nearly one year to complete.

6
Parham Santana also created comprehensive style guides to help licensing partners and retailers around the world adhere to the newly created standards.

5

6

1998 EDITION

DeLORME

New Features
• 1998 AAA TourBook Data
• DeLorme Slide Show
• Easy Dashboard Interface

Award-Winning MAPS

AAA
Map 'n' Go
FROM AMERICA'S #1 TRAVEL PLANNER

$100 worth of Travel Coupons Included

• Put the fun back into road trips!
• Create your perfect route
• Detailed, accurate maps

DeLORME

AAA
Map 'n' Go
Plan the Perfect Vacation
→ Includes over 66,000 1999 AAA-approved lodgings, restaurants, campgrounds and attractions
→ Easy-to-use features for fun on the road

ging
age)
tory
nish
ny's
dn't
or a
able
helf.

DeLorme Design Process

DeLorme, a quirky former atlas publisher in Yarmouth, Maine, pioneered digital mapping technology in the 1980s, when they introduced Street Atlas USA, the first software to chart every street in America on a CD-ROM. Opening endless possibilities with this software, the company began paving the way into business-to-business products and, most recently, GPS solutions for portable devices.

REASON FOR REDESIGN

Since it introduced its first software line in the late 1980s, DeLorme had not redesigned its packaging. On chaotic consumer-software shelves, the packages weren't hitting their mark. In addition, DeLorme had expanded into a number of other software packages and versions, and there was no consistent scheme to tie together the different brands and products. Finally, the illustration style represented on the boxes was somewhat cartoonish and did not visually describe the product capabilities.

REDESIGN OBJECTIVES

- Find a discernable look that DeLorme could own for its software packaging
- Clear the way for a more complex and structured product offering
- Reinforce DeLorme as a technology innovator while making the software look fun and easy to use

THE RESULTS

In an extremely competitive retail environment, DeLorme continues to thrive. The consistent look created by creative firm LMS Design has prevailed on all the company's software packaging, including newly released products for handheld computers.

1

2

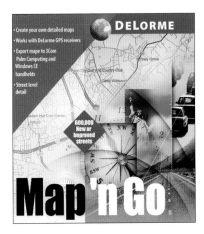

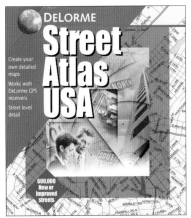

1, 2
LMS Design began exploring a montage of images that added rich texture and sophistication to the packaging's face. The images also more immediately conveyed the purpose of the product inside the box.

3–5
The Final design maintained the integrity of the brand while achieving its objectives, outlined early in the redesign process.

6
The final design maintained the integrity of the brand while achieving its objectives outlined early in the redesign process.

3

4

5

6

Lionel Trains

DESIGN
One Zero Charlie, Greenwood, Illinois
MARKET
Worldwide

before

Lionel Trains, founded in 1900, enjoyed a golden age in the 1940s and early 1950s. The trains' packaging then featured clean, Art Deco–inspired type and handsome blocks of color that characterized the model trains' visual brand. The style carried through all of the company's packaging and its logo.

The final packaging revived the same bold, classy look of Lionel's glory days, with a sleek, modern edge.

Lionel Design Process

The story of Lionel, the century-old manufacturer of America's most treasured model trains, is one as rocky and astounding as the American twentieth century itself. Founded in 1903, the little company in a cramped office in New York City turned out the first B&O No. 5 electric locomotive. A few years later, Lionel invented the preassembled toy train track, steam locomotives, and a selection of cars powered by 110-volt electric transformers, giving birth to the concept of the model train that we know today.

After that first momentous decade, the company rode the waves of prosperity, depression, and war. It also survived the demise of the railroad and held its own against the competing boyhood fascination with space-themed toys and, later, video games. The founder sold the company in the late 1950s, around the time that trains' former glory was fading. The company declared bankruptcy, then licensed its manufacturing to food company General Mills, which later outsourced the manufacturing to Mexico. Two years later, the manufacturing returned to its home base in Michigan, but the company changed hands again in 1995.

Despite what was going on within the company, Lionel continued to innovate: introducing and improving upon classics that, although not as in demand for youngsters, captured the imagination and loyalty of hundreds of thousands of adult collectors around the world.

REASON FOR REDESIGN

All these changes left the company and its visual brand in shambles. Trademarks, package designs, catalogs, and other printed collateral were piecemeal and rarely recalled the company's "visual equity or heritage." This was a must for a product like Lionel—especially considering the tireless attention to aesthetic detail in the product design over the years. As a result, formerly loyal customers saw the product quality as deteriorating because they no longer related to the brand visuals.

Lionel's creative firm One Zero Charlie embarked on a sweeping brand restoration project for Lionel. Instead of depending on market research and focus groups (which the client and designers saw as the source of so many intermittent and off-target changes over the years), the designers relied on the intuition and vision of the company's new, strong leadership— including rock star Neil Young, the company's co-owner.

"Neil, with no MBA degree, marketing, or business background, needless to say, was not inclined to follow traditional thinking," says One Zero Charlie's creative director Michael Stanard. "His strong personality, combined with our firm's intuitive feel for the Lionel heritage, carried the day. In brief, we just rocked."

REDESIGN OBJECTIVES

- Refresh and restore the Lionel brand to elevate the company and its products to their former glory
- Explore cost savings in the structural packaging production
- Address the pervasive problem of product returns due to damaged packaging

THE RESULTS

The packaging's new look eloquently narrates Lionel's rich history of innovative design. At the same time, it changed the assembly-line production, which resulted in substantial cost savings. And the train sets' physical packaging better protects the product, leading to fewer product returns and happier retailers.

1

2

3

5

1, 2
By the 1970s, sadly, Lionel's original look had all but eroded. Occasionally, a box included an allusion to the old logo (2, from 1989). However, every box was different—packaging for different trains used their own permutations of a logo—and background colors and images varied wildly.

3–5
When One Zero Charlie took on the Lionel project, they set out to restore Lionel's visual brand. Along the way, they established a hierarchy of logos, referring to the most important pieces of the constantly evolving logos through the years. Ultimately, the merit badge logo (4), the one closest to Lionel's 1950s design, became the brand's primary emblem.

6, 7
Other, secondary logos were then created for special product series.

8
One challenge the One Zero Charlie and Lionel teams faced was making the packaging sturdier, because one of retailers' biggest complaints was the number of returns due to product damage.

6

7

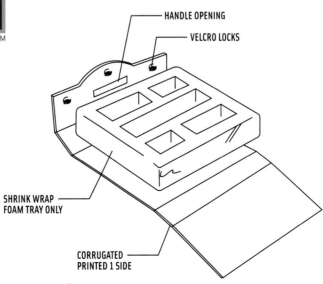

HANDLE OPENING

VELCRO LOCKS

SHRINK WRAP
FOAM TRAY ONLY

CORRUGATED
PRINTED 1 SIDE

8

Secrets of Success

PRESERVE EXISTING BRAND EQUITIES

When a manufacturer decides its venerable brand needs a makeover, designers must walk a fine line between an effective, contemporary design and an unsettling makeover that confuses or turns off faithful consumers.

"DON'T MESS IT UP!"

That's the mantra of Michael Osborne, principal of Michael Osborne Design, when his team approaches modernizing makeovers of well-known brands. "We start every project by discovering what the equity items are—what needs to be retained, and how much room is there for change," Osborne says.

Consumers have an emotional history with a package, no matter how old and dusty the product is. Realistically evaluating what consumers still relate to—and what isn't pushing the brand forward, even if it appeals nostalgically to consumers—helps you decide what to build from in the new iteration. In the case of outdated packaging, companies typically decide on a more evolutionary approach to keep a brand fresh but familiar.

SET EXPECTATIONS ABOUT RESULTS EARLY ON

Experts say it's unrealistic to expect dramatic sales increases due to packaging redesigns, especially projects meant to refresh a brand and keep it contemporary. While most clients might realize that from the get-go, it's a designer's responsibility to make sure clients' desired outcomes of redesign projects are realistic.

Postredesign research might show improved consumer perception or product visibility even if sales don't jump noticeably, says Scott Young, president of Perception Research Services in Fort Lee, New Jersey. Those kinds of results show success for an outdated packaging's redesign—they signify that the refresh helps to keep a product in the forefront of people's minds.

KNOW YOUR DEMOGRAPHICS (NOW, NOT THEN)

Understand that your target consumers are different than they were a generation ago—and depending on the product, even a few years ago seems like a generation—and so is the retail environment in which they're buying the product. Even if it's an exercise that your client conducted only a couple of years ago, and even if the manufacturer insists it knows its customers, it never hurts to step back and study the people the product is for and those shopper's contemporary experiences both in and out of the retail store.

before / after

Don't mess with a good thing: Jack Daniels
The redesign of Jack Daniels whiskey by Michael Osborne Design in 2003 was the revered liquor's first refresh in years, conducted as more whiskey brands began to crowd the store shelves. The manufacturer knew that customers would panic at anything more than a barely noticeable refresh, so the JD redesign meant subtle typeface changes to the raised lettering on the glass bottle, and an even less perceptible remolding of the bottle's shape.

before

after

Brand equity is king: Carlos V

Nestlé Mexico's Carlos V candy bar had been on the market since 1955, and many adults with children and grandchildren of their own knew the brand well. The candy's brown wrapper, with a stripe of red tying it to the Nestlé brand, featured an old-fashioned illustration of a stodgy king. After market research showed adults saw the brand as tired, Nestlé asked creative firm TD2 to investigate "killing the king" and mimicking imported brands. Instead, TD2 defended the king—the packaging's distinguishing feature—and rethought the target audience: kids, not adults. Redrawn into a dashing, Disney-style character, the Carlos V king, along with the other new design details, sent sales soaring by 30 percent.

Old Spice

DESIGN
Interbrand, New York, New York
MARKET
Worldwide

The Old Spice brand and the packaging design, which had been on the market for decades, lagged well behind modern times. The logo was old-fashioned and the text was blocky and unimpressive. The manufacturer and branding firm Interbrand sought a strategy for modernizing the brand and appealing to younger consumers while retaining important elements of the strong brand equity.

The new packaging design is handsome, classic, and appealing across demograph[...]. The new Old Spice combines the original brand's timelessness with a bold, contem[...]rary, masculine look.

Old Spice Design Process

On the market for decades, Old Spice was an internationally recognized brand, known as much as the dependable Father's Day gift by generations of children as by the over-forty-five consumer base that faithfully purchased the aftershave lotion. But though the brand captured an emotional connection among consumers of all ages—whether the men who still purchased it, those who first shaved using it, or those who bought it for holidays and birthdays for beloved fathers and grandfathers— Old Spice was not attracting the young male consumer that manufacturer Procter & Gamble wanted to reach.

REASON FOR REDESIGN

Procter & Gamble had a surprisingly enduring brand on its hands (some participants in market research studies could still sing the Old Spice jingle from three decades before) and wanted to stand behind it, yet open the doors to new market opportunities. The company worked with Interbrand to research ways in which they could revitalize the brand. Early studies, however, proved that moving the old logomark to new packaging wouldn't be enough—no matter how they sliced it, the Old Spice brand was not working in modern times. Interbrand set out to help the company rebrand Old Spice in a way that would inspire and appeal to young males without alienating the older, loyal customer.

REDESIGN OBJECTIVES

- Rebrand Old Spice for success, boosting it to the number one male grooming product set in the world
- Appeal to a new demographic, primarily the young, casual, down-to-earth man, using new colors, type, and graphics with which the target consumer could identify
- Elevate the brand to a modern, higher-class image so its products could ultimately move into a higher price point

THE RESULTS

Old Spice has become one of Procter & Gamble's fastest-growing brands since the relaunch of the new packaging. Within months after the launch, Old Spice jumped to the number one brand of antiperspirant among teenage boys and leapt several notches to take its place among the top-rated male grooming brands in the world.

1

2

3

1

Early research convinced the Interbrand team that the ship logo was too familiar to abandon—many consumers could still sing the sea shanty jingle from 1970s and 1980s TV commercials for Old Spice.

2

Interbrand worried that a quick facelift would still leave an out-of-date brand, and that it wouldn't do justice to the strength of the product. The designers began drafting concepts for a contemporary, "unapologetically masculine" new look that would appeal to young men. They redesigned Old Spice's antiperspirant line first, the idea being that a subbrand would be safer to launch first. Once the success of the new branding was confirmed, it could be applied to the brand at large.

3

Designers explored different ways to change the logo and typefaces—balancing the need to still speak to over-forty-five male consumers who were the loyalists while adding a young, masculine flavor to the image. They also transformed the logo from a three-masted clipper ship—the stuff of old-time pirate movies—to a sleek, contemporary sloop.

4

Once the design was successfully imple-mented in one subbrand, Interbrand and manufacturer Procter & Gamble extended it across the product line, building a pack-aging system that would work for existing and new products.

US GD-3 DEODORANT (also in Canada) Two Sizes - 2.25oz and 3.25oz

US GS - 3.0 oz INVISIBLE SOLID ANTI-PERSPIRANT/DEODORANT (also in Canada)

US BODY SPRAY - 4.0 oz (also in Canada)

US CLEAR GEL ANTI-PERSPIRANT/DEODORANT - 3.0 oz (also in Canada)

US "M" ANTI-PERSPIRANT/DEODORANT (also in Canada) Two Sizes - 1.7oz and 2.6oz (Unscented only 2.6 oz)

US Classic DEODORANT - Two Sizes - 2.25oz and 3.25oz

US Classic DEODORANT Round Stick

US Classic APDO Stick

4

before

[The] original packaging for
[LensCrafters] was based on the old
[tag line] promising service in one hour.
[Since] this claim was becoming
[common] among optical stores,
[LensCrafters] decided to shift its
[emphasis] toward promoting its line
[of eye]wear, and needed pack-
[aging that ec]hoed this new direction.

The end packaging kept the combination of positive and negative circles as its design motif. The colorful box sliding into the white bag work together to communicate a unified brand personality, and also makes the unwrapping of the glasses more of a "nested" discovery process.

LensCrafters Design Process

LensCrafters is the largest optical retail chain in the world, with more than 850 stores across the United States and Canada. A subsidiary of the Italian optical luxury group Luxottica, owner of brands as diverse as Versace, Ray Ban, and Sunglass Hut, LensCrafters achieved success by consolidating all aspects of shopping for eyewear or contact lenses into a single package. Customers can get their eyes examined by an optometrist, consult with an optician, and choose fashion-forward frames in a single place. But the chain's true success came from its well-known brand positioning that prevailed throughout the company's early years: a place to get quality eyeglasses made onsite in about an hour.

REASON FOR REDESIGN

Over the years, however, many of LensCrafters' competitors could also make the one-hour claim. The chain wanted to move away from being simply a clinic and laboratory to becoming a showroom—a place offering ongoing optical care, but also a place where customers could come to shop for eyeglasses as an accessory rather than a necessity. To help recreate its image, LensCrafters commissioned Chute Gerdeman to rethink its brand, including its packaging design.

The existing packaging consisted of little more than a two-color polybag, a mall-store shopping bag meant to hold manufacturers' cases customers received with their new glasses. The new packaging would create more of a fluid brand experience.

REDESIGN OBJECTIVES

- Create new packaging structures to better immerse products in LensCrafters branding
- Design a youthful, fun feeling to appeal to a broad demographic
- Build a brand personality to remind customers that purchasing eyeglasses is less of a medical need, and more of a personal statement

THE RESULTS

At press time, LensCrafters had released the new packaging design in select markets. Based on favorable results, the chain has plans to roll out the new design nationwide.

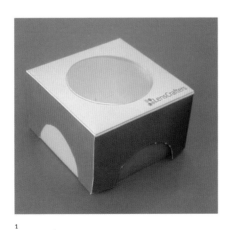

1

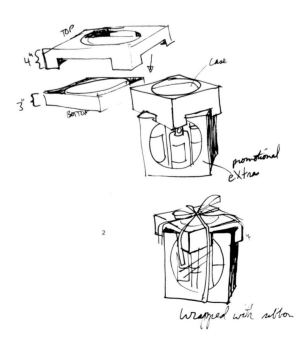

2

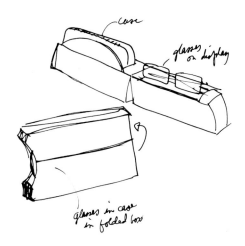

case

glasses on display

glasses in case in folded box

3

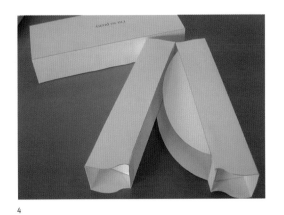

4

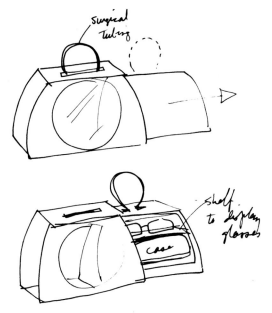

surgical tubing

shelf to display glasses

case

5

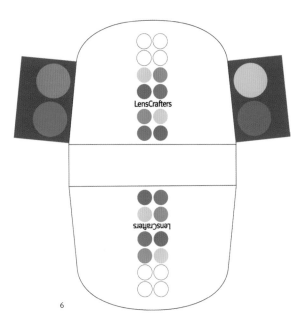

LensCrafters

LensCrafters

6

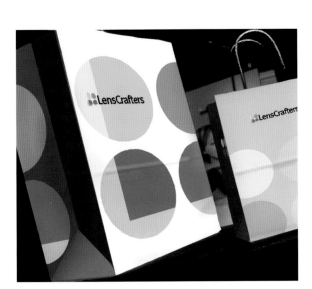

LensCrafters

LensCrafters

7

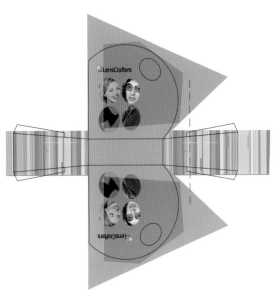

LensCrafters

LensCrafters

8

1, 2
The designers set out to create innovative new structures as well as new graphic treatments. Here, a "platform" box includes a two-part top that holds glasses and a case, and could be combined with a promotional item to create a presentation bundle.

3, 4
The idea for the "stapler" box involved a box that fully opens to display glasses with the brand case—a way to surround manufacturer-branded products with the LensCrafter brand.

5, 6
A "bowling bag" packaging idea conceptualized a shelf to hold the glasses and their case, which would then slide into a sleeve to act like a carrying case.

7, 8
Picking up elements of the new LensCrafter logo, four multicolored dots, these bag concepts used bright colors, circular shapes, and young, funky photographs that represented fashionable shoppers.

Bamboo Inc., Minneapolis, Minnesota

ART DIRECTOR AND DESIGNER
Kathy Soranno, Bamboo

COPYWRITER
Judy Soranno, Bamboo

Ellie Kingsbury

MARKET
United States (Minnesota)

before

Schroeder's milk cartons had
remained unchanged since the
1970s, when the company targeted
primarily the price-point convenience
store market. Sporting stale colors
and outdated graphics, the milk
cartons still suggested an aging,
unsophisticated small business.
In fact, Schroeder had an impressive
story of innovation and technological
expertise that no consumer could infer
from its musty shelf presence. Also,
no consistent architecture existed
from variety to variety.

cereal sold separately

SKIM MILK

VITAMIN A&D
FAT FREE / GRADE A

HALF GALLON (1.89L)

SCHRØDER

skim

cookies not included

1% LOWFAT MILK

VITAMIN A&D
1% MILKFAT / GRADE A

HALF GALLON (1.89L)

SCHRØDER

one

pour, drink, repeat

REDUCED FAT MILK 2%

2% LESS FAT
THAN WHOLE MILK
VITAMIN A&D
2% MILKFAT / GRADE A

HALF GALLON (1.89L)

SCHRØDER

two

sharing not necessary

WHOLE MILK

VITAMIN A&D
GRADE A

HALF GALLON (1.89L)

SCHRØDER

whole

Schroeder Milk Design Process

Running to the corner store for a carton of milk late at night usually doesn't involve a lot of thought: You reach for the first half-gallon you see, perhaps drifting toward the carton whose color or old-fashioned script seems most familiar.

Schroeder Milk wanted to change all that. In the early 1990s, the Minnesota-based, family-owned dairy, in business for 118 years, still packaged their dairy-case staples in cartons designed in the 1970s, when the company was marketing heavily to regional convenience stores. The brand that emerged did little to promote the tradition of innovation, technology, and quality on which the company prided itself.

REASON FOR REDESIGN

When Jill Schroeder became brand manager in 1993, she identified opportunities to expand into the high-end grocery market by reinventing the brand's retail image. Making the attributes of the company—and the product—inherent in the packaging design was key to this initiative.

Another consideration was a practical one: The company wanted to protect the milk from light and the depletion of vitamins, minerals, and flavor, as well as cater to the needs of busy families with a package that was resealable and portable. New plastic containers were part of the company's drive to bring Schroeder Milk into the twenty-first century.

REDESIGN OBJECTIVES

- Communicate brand attributes—technological innovation and top quality—on the package
- Create a fun design that was much different than anything else happening in dairy, to emphasize the uniqueness of the Schroeder product
- Add an element of fun that made a powerful personality statement by differentiating Schroeder's from other dairy brands
- Create a new packaging system for easier identification of the brand and its varieties, for an overall more functional container

THE RESULTS

Since the initial launch, Schroeder has reported a 12 percent increase in overall sales, and sales of the company's new on-the-go compact pints have grown by 30 percent. In addition to winning important new accounts representing premium grocers, Schroeder and its creative firm Bamboo received prestigious nods from the design community, including awards from *ID* magazine, IDFA, the Beverage Packaging Global Design Awards, and the London International Design Awards.

1

2

3

1
Schroeder and its creative firm, Bamboo, decided to defy the rules and go far beyond a simple face-lift. The company wanted to completely rebrand itself, primarily by exploring a look for its logo and packaging that was unlike anything else in the dairy case. Bamboo studied dairy packaging from all over the world and discovered that images of cows and farms were almost without fail the adopted symbols of dairy, like the Schroeder logo itself.

2
The designers took a 180-degree approach, eliminating Schroeder's old, rural farmhouse identity. Instead, they explored a clean, modern wordmark that stood out as distinctive and memorable.

3
As part of the initiative, Schroeder decided to switch to an opaque white plastic container to preserve freshness. The final design approach, chosen by Schroeder and strongly recommended by Bamboo, made the white a prominent part of the design, symbolizing a purity and simplicity that wordlessly summed up the product inside.

4
Creating a crystal-clear classification, the designers spelled out the varieties (1%, 2%, skim, and whole) in bright, friendly colors and set them on their sides with matching lids. The words are easy to read yet still unique in their placement and color. Compared to the original packaging, the company's name is also more prominent.

5
Consumers can locate the milk—no matter what size or variety they want—right away. Compared to agricultural-minded competitors in cardboard cartons, the Schroeder containers are bold and different. Even on in-store banners, funny sayings jab at consumers' milk-buying "personality" preferences.

4

5

Tsar

Tsar

DESIGN
Curiosity Inc., Tokyo, Japan
MARKET
Worldwide

before

Van Cleef & Arpel's Tsar, though still a distinguished men's fragrance, paled next to its more modern competitors when it came to its packaging. The bottle still retained hints of an '80s-style design—marbled green box, musty gold and green accents, and lightly printed type—which reduced the bottle's impact by modern standards.

The f
betw
and

Tsar Design Process

Luxury goods purveyor Van Cleef & Arpels has sold Tsar, a sporty men's fragrance with hints of pineapple, thyme, lavender, and patchouli, since 1998. With the powerful Van Cleef name behind it, Tsar stands among the higher-end designer fragrances on the market.

REASON FOR REDESIGN

The packaging, both the box and bottle, were nondescript. The plain box with lightly printed lettering was dated and did nothing to help the product stand out among the dozens of other designer fragrances available for men, let alone define the product as a leader in modern luxury. Van Cleef & Arpels approached creative firm Curiosity Inc. to find a way to express the product's timelessness while still communicating modernity.

REDESIGN OBJECTIVES

- Strengthen the product image as top quality
- Reinforce Tsar's originality and modernity while conveying its timelessness
- Create a quality package that would be rich in texture while keeping the materials simple enough to keep costs down

THE RESULTS

Consumer magazines dubbed Tsar a "modern classic" following the 2002 packaging redesign.

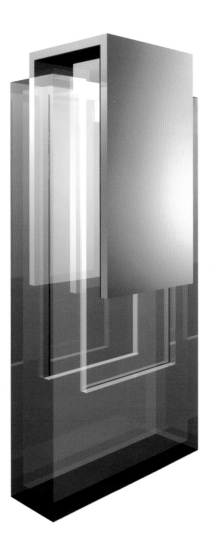

1

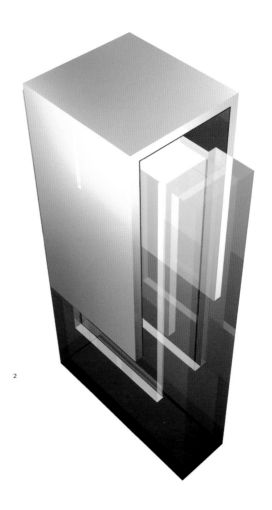

2

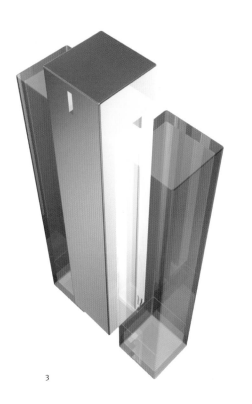

1, 2
Creative firm Curiosity Inc. aimed to build a bottle that applied Tsar's existing brand assets (namely, the color green) with a design rich in texture and dimension. They presented a number of concepts based on the use of transparent green glass. In this concept, the bottle bursts outward in a complex, multidimensional structure.

3, 4
Another concept involved three units linked together, with the bottle pump supported by two bold legs of green glass.

5, 6
In its final concept, Curiosity explored the idea of using wavy glass for a uniquely textured bottle. The client pursued this idea, sending the designers on a mission to explore the most cost efficient and successful way to execute this highly specialized technique. Curiosity's biggest challenges lay in researching how the rippled glass would ultimately look on the store shelves, as well as making sure the green color was consistent across the surface of the bottle.

7
Lined up together, the bottles make an impressive cavalry of distinguished light and color.

3

4

5

6

7

Changing Faces:
REDESIGNING TO REMAIN COMPETITIVE

before

The former Aveeno packaging (right, shown next to the newly designed moisturizing lotion bottle) was blocky and had a surprisingly masculine feel in its rigid angularity. It was also easy for retail stores to mimic in their private-label product packaging. Finally, the product's look fell in line with lower-priced competing skin-care products, whereas Johnson & Johnson hoped to elevate Aveeno to a higher-end category.

The final packaging went a long way
to shake up the skin- and face-care
categories in Aveeno's price range—
a unique, memorable shape and a b
logo that still makes an impression
natural softness and class.

Aveeno Design Process

Over many years, Aveeno became a household name when generations of kids slathered on the lotion to ease itching from chicken pox. The formula of natural colloidal oatmeal was a soothing, anti-itch remedy approved by medical professionals and appreciated by mothers.

The product had long been owned by S. C. Johnson, which had kept the product virtually the same. When Johnson & Johnson bought the Aveeno line in 1999, the company realized it was sitting on a gold mine: a line of products that spanned the categories in a drugstore and represented tremendous consumer recognition and untapped potential.

REASON FOR REDESIGN

Johnson & Johnson saw the opportunity to relaunch Aveeno as a higher-end natural skin-care line, sliding neatly into a niche that was different than products like Johnson & Johnson's Neutrogena line. Realizing that Aveeno had practically become a generic product in the marketplace, the manufacturer and creative firm LMS latched onto the concept of "active natural" for Aveeno and set out to built a brand worthy of higher retail prices in the drugstore skin-care category.

REDESIGN OBJECTIVES

- Relaunch Aveeno as a higher-end natural skin-care brand, leveraging the product's existing reputation and consumer familiarity
- Create an ownable bottle structure that felt feminine and set Aveeno apart from other products
- Stay several steps ahead of the drugstore private brands, making a large enough departure from the existing product that the generic competitors would have a hard time mimicking the new look

THE RESULTS

According to Johnson & Johnson's financial results, their consumer products division sales have enjoyed strong growth, fueled strongly in part by its skin care line, of which Aveeno is one of the three major brands. The company has stood behind the line with new product launches and promotions.

1

2

3

4

5

6

7

1–3
One of the first ways that LMS Design combined the dual needs of a proprietary design and a more stylized approach was to investigate a different bottle design. Bottles with sleek curves and rounded edges not only would help Aveeno stand out from the competition but offered a softer design to appeal to the product's female consumers.

4
In the bottle's graphics, the designers wanted to appeal to women but also emphasize Aveeno's natural ingredients—the brand's major selling point for decades.

5, 6
Speckled, oatmeal-colored designs were another attempt to refer to Aveeno's long history as a trusted, oatmeal-based anti-itch remedy. Simple, pretty graphics added a distinctly feminine touch.

7, 8
The design direction that the client finally chose involved a more sophisticated approach that still incorporated natural images. The designers then applied that approach to the Aveeno skin-care line packaging.

8

Clearly Canadian

DESIGN
Karacters Design Group, Vancouver,
British Columbia, Canada
LEAD DESIGNER AND ASSOCIATE CREATIVE DIRECTOR
Matthew Clark
CREATIVE DIRECTOR
Maria Kennedy
PATTERN DESIGNERS
Michelle Melenchuk, Roy White, Jeff Harrison,
Nancy Wu, Marsha Kupsch, Kara Bohl, Ken Therrien,
Matthew Clark

PROJECT MANAGER
Brynn Wanstall
SENIOR PRODUCER
John Ziros
COMPUTER PRODUCTION
Lisa Good and Peter Hall
PRINTER
Seallt, Inc
MARKET
North America

before

The original design of Clearly Canadian's bottles was the freshest thing on the beverage market when it came out in 1988—it was a breath of fresh air next to its competition, which was mostly nationally branded colas. A minimal redesign by Karacters in 1995 attempted to improve some functional attributes (deeper-blue bottle, more visible type, more dramatic fruit images) to help the brand stand out on the shelf. But four years later, this phenomenon of alternative beverages was lagging behind newcomers to the category. The manufacturer needed to rethink its presentation for an increasingly fickle, fashion-conscious consumer, prompting a 1999 redesign.

The 2002 relaunch picked up wh[...]
last design left off, with the same [...]
colors, and added rich patterns to [...]
the essence of each flavor. "Each [...]
is composed of three solid ink co[...]
down like a silk-screen print to c[...]
textural quality," explains former [...]
associate creative director Matthe[...]
The brilliant new bottles are pro[...]
as fashion accessories.

Clearly Canadian Design Process

Clearly Canadian, along with emerging brands such as Snapple, led the invention of the alternative beverages category in the late '80s with their colorless, carbonated fruit drinks. The beverage became synonymous with hip, giving stylish consumers an artistic bottle, interesting new flavors, and a health-conscious alternative to sugary sodas. Over the years, the category became extremely crowded, however, as more brands rolled out new juice and tea formulas in outlandish bottles designed to scream from the store shelves.

REASON FOR REDESIGN

By 1999, Clearly Canadian was paling next to the category's young newcomers. Market research showed consumers had grown weary of the brand's bottle shape and no longer saw the blue glass as unique. The audience for this category is famously adventurous (and fickle), and the brand's image wasn't drawing a crowd anymore. What followed is legendary: Karacters Design Group redesigned the brand radically in 1999, winning design accolades and increasing bottle sales after the relaunch from 10 million to 30 million in the first quarter alone.

Clearly Canadian learned its lesson after the first redesign experience, and, in 2002, they returned for a refresh. Realizing that its target consumer approaches beverage selection as a veritable fashion accessory, the company knew it was already time to update.

REDESIGN OBJECTIVES

- Communicate flavor other than with fruit images (which consumers had difficulty accepting)
- Play up the bold flavors and more clearly distinguish different flavors from one another
- Feature Clearly Canadian's unique clear, carbonated formulation
- Create an innovative design that would bowl over fashion- and design-conscious consumers

THE RESULTS

The 2002 refresh gave retail sales a shot in the arm. Retailers overwhelmingly renewed orders and, in some cases, expanded their offerings of the beverage line, and consumer awareness shot up again.

1

2

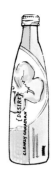

3

EXPERIMENTAL PACKAGING

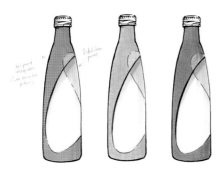

4

5

6

7

8

1–3
In 1999, Clearly Canadian teamed up with Karacters Design Group to study a new direction for the bottles. Karacters learned that consumers had tired of the blue-glass bottle (assumed to be a critical feature of the brand). Nothing was sacred as Karacters Design Group set out to explore new treatments for the bottle. They presented Clearly Canadian with a number of different sketches based on current design trends of the time and different positioning concepts, from lucid simplicity to crazy prints.

4, 5
The company latched onto the idea of a bold color identifying the flavor, as an expression of "big taste" instead of literal "fruit." Karacters experimented with a new, modern-looking logo that prominently displays the product name and symbolizes the effervescence of the beverage.

6
The final design that launched in 1999 was as classy and unique as the old bottles had once been. To execute this design, Karacters looked to a shrink-film label, which covered the bottle with a flexible, sculptural look while still offering a frosted window into the bottle so consumers could see the clear liquid inside (an unusual application—shrink film traditionally is used to hide the interior of a bottle). The new design won the company and Karacters a number of prestigious design awards.

7, 8
Only two years later, with a new understanding of its target consumers' evolving tastes, Clearly Canadian returned to Karacters for a refresh. This time, the goal was not to salvage the brand but to help it stay ahead of the pack with a package that was also a piece of art. For this redesign, Karacters returned to some its original, more extreme concepts presented during the first redesign process.

Epson America and its creative firm, SooHoo Designers, studied Epson products' shelf presence compared to that of its competition. What they discovered was outdated graphics, a packaging system that wasn't unified, and a weak overall brand image.

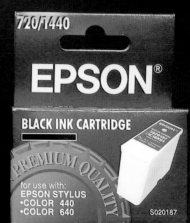

The redesigned packaging more prominently emphasizes vibrant photography to tell the product's story, while images of the product itself play a secondary role.

Epson Design Process

A division of the Japanese giant Seiko-Epson, the Epson brand has been associated with printer technology and computing since the 1970s. In more recent years, Epson America's lines of affordable, personal inkjet printers and accompanying ink cartridges have been its bread and butter in Western Hemisphere markets. To differentiate itself, the company has taken up the torch to bring digital imaging into consumers' homes. However, Epson America needed to better communicate why it stood out against the similarly strong brands that flanked its products in electronics stores.

REASON FOR REDESIGN

Epson America and its creative firm, SooHoo Designers, compared the current packaging to competitors' to determine how Epson's shelf presence measured up. They found that the packaging looked dated and didn't convey Epson's status as a leader in digital technology and imaging.

Although the creative team established objectives for helping Epson increase brand recognition, it was also challenged with finding a way to create new packaging that could keep up with fast-to-market products and to reduce design, production, and printing costs.

REDESIGN OBJECTIVES

- Lower Epson's package production costs and decrease production time
- Increase brand awareness
- Help Epson stand out from the competition

THE RESULTS

The packaging launched throughout the entire Western Hemisphere, giving Epson products a distinctive and recognizable face to the world. Though Epson America has not disclosed sales results since the packaging debut, the company is very pleased with the performance of packaging at the retail level.

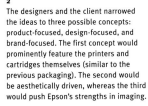

1
SooHoo Designers explored all possible approaches to a new packaging system. Initial ideas ranged from overblown type announcing the product name to artistic renderings of the printers.

2
The designers and the client narrowed the ideas to three possible concepts: product-focused, design-focused, and brand-focused. The first concept would prominently feature the printers and cartridges themselves (similar to the previous packaging). The second would be aesthetically driven, whereas the third would push Epson's strengths in imaging.

3
The SooHoo team and Epson America senior management met to refine each direction, then tested comps of the directions in focus groups. After they received all the input, the team reached the conclusion that all consumers wanted the same things out of the products: ease of use, speed, and great image quality. The team decided to adopt the image-focused direction.

2

3

Secrets of Success

You could argue that competition plays a role in any packaging redesign—or a brand project or advertising campaign, for that matter. At the end of the day, it's all about selling more than the other guy, gaining market share, and earning profits. But sometimes, competition is the primary reason for a package redesign: Competitors are crowding the brand out of the market, and it's time for the brand to fight back.

TAKE SEVERAL STRIDES FORWARD

Especially in categories where competing brands adopt a me-too approach, brands need to move far enough ahead with their designs that it's difficult, financially and creatively, for copycats to catch up. Such was the case with Johnson & Johnson's Aveeno. Private-label products in some drug and retail stores were being designed to resemble the old Aveeno bottle.

The resulting redesign is often a substantial departure from the original and often involves discovering a characteristic that is unique to the client.

HOW IS IT DIFFERENT?

In the same vein, many times clients may be challenged with making a clear-cut statement about what makes them different from the other major brands in their category. This exercise can be truly challenging, particularly when only a handful of major players exist in any one space. Companies and their creative teams must make sure all the components are working together—the packaging supporting the advertising, which supports the point-of-purchase materials, and so on—to ensure that statement sticks.

SooHoo Designers, for instance, worked to establish Epson as the digital imaging champion with the brand's system of colorful, image-driven packaging.

SHAKE UP THE CATEGORY

One way to generate excitement is to set the bar higher than ever within a category by doing something very different. This is not to say that designers should select an outlandish or faddish design that will pale once the sizzle wears off; rather, they should reevaluate the established standards for packaging in their product's realm.

before

after

The applicator bottle for Insignia deodorant, marketed in the United Kingdom, was old and tired looking. The competition for the brand used hard, dark graphics and colors, so the designers at Lippa Pearce Design tried a completely different approach to help the deodorant cut through the noise. Lippa Pearce applied natural, abstract images and an idiosyncratic *i* for a young, quirky look aimed at sixteen-to-twenty-five-year-old males. The new package was a big hit in the U.K. market.

Lipovitan

DESIGN
Blackburn's Design, London, United Kingdom
MARKET
United Kingdom and Europe

before

The previous Lipovitan can had a lot going on: differently shaped graphics of mechanical cogs, an array of icons, and product information presented somewhat haphazardly around the can. The drink's packaging didn't seem to be appealing to the manufacturer's target demographic in the European market: twenty-five to forty-four-year-old health-conscious consumers, especially in the United Kingdom.

LIPOVITAN

after

The sleek, blue Lipovitan Vitality can presents a sense of youthful energy but with a pureness and serenity that appeals to people who like to treat their bodies well.

LIPOVITAN

Lipovitan Design Process

Lipovitan is an energy health drink by Japan's largest over-the-counter pharmaceutical company, Taisho. The brand has been on the market since the 1960s, though with many different formulations, and was the first beverage of its kind—a natural health and energy drink.

A couple of years ago, the company conducted widespread market research and determined an opportunity for a natural energy drink for the twenty-five to forty-five demographic, especially in the U.K. and European markets. In 2003, Taisho relaunched the beverage as Lipovitan Vitality, a drink containing almost the total recommended daily allowance of vitamins B1, B2, B3, and B6, plus herbal ingredients such as royal jelly and ginseng, but less caffeine and sugar than competitors such as Red Bull and Lucozade.

REASON FOR REDESIGN

Lipovitan's old can was outdated and somewhat unremarkable, with a confusing hierarchy, muddy colors, and graphics to which European consumers didn't seem to relate. The manufacturer wanted Lipovitan to stand out as a friendly, natural, modern energy drink that promoted overall well-being, hoping this image would help the drink gain ground over competing brands that took a more aggressive approach.

REDESIGN OBJECTIVES

- Increase consumer product awareness at the point of purchase
- Redefine positioning in a way that would be understandable and appealing to consumers
- Ultimately boost Lipovitan to the number two slot in the energy drink category, after Red Bull

THE RESULTS

The manufacturer backed the new launch with a great deal of advertising, and the new brand and its package earned substantial press coverage, earning Lipovitan increased market share.

LIPOVITAN

1

LIPOVITAN
VITALITY

LIPOVITAN
VITALITY

2

3

4

5

6

1
Blackburn's Design in London began looking at how Lipovitan's manufacturer could update and improve on the packaging. The first target was the blocky logo, which was too heavy and uninviting for a health drink.

2
Blackburn's devised a lighter, friendlier logo with a distinctive and ownable look—specifically, the raised *V*, which served double duty as a built-in pronunciation guide for consumers not familiar with the brand.

3
The floating cogs on the original package were meant to symbolize the way in which vitamins worked together to fuel the body, as in a machine. But the symbols were confusing. The main cog was actually oval-shaped on the can, whereas real-life cogs are perfectly round. And the smaller cogs floated independent of one another. Blackburn's designers re-created the cogs and locked them together to demonstrate the way the three main vitamins collaborated to release energy.

4
Designers then investigated the best ways to represent the brand using the revitalized cog symbols. Ideas included a simple, modern look; a watercolor allusion to natural ingredients; more literal references to nature with wildlife images in the cogs; and a rendering of old-time strongmen to represent stamina and strength.

5
Inspired by da Vinci, the designers began going down the path of using different forms of the human body. These symbols would be understood internationally, and everyone could relate to them. They also helped convey different emotions and states of mind, which was important for a multitasking energy and health drink.

6
The designers suspended the body forms in varying states of activity within the circular cogs, using pleasant shades of blue for harmony.

Sackets Harbor War of 1812 Ale

DESIGN
Iron Design, Ithaca, New York
MARKET
United States (upstate New York)

The bottles for War of 1812 Ale that had been in circulation since 1999 referred quite literally to the history behind the microbrew's name: a pen-and-ink drawing of a majestic ship inside a ring displaying the brewery's name. A green banner flying beneath the insignia featured the War of 1812 Ale name. Although the design was faithful to the brand name's history, it wasn't helping the regionally focused microbrew compete against better-known New England–branded beers, such as Samuel Adams.

The new bottles, launched in June 2003, reach out to younger beer drinkers who still treasure the heritage of local microbrews. Iron Design also redesigned the tap handle to draw a parallel between the bottles in retail stores and the beer on draught.

Sackets Harbor War of 1812 Ale
Design Process

Sackets Harbor Brewing Company is a local microbrewery in upstate New York. Though the restaurant and pub has been around only since the mid-1990s, word has spread about the beer it brews—War of 1812 Ale—largely because of the pub's location in the touristy Thousand Islands region. After only a year in business, the pub outgrew its onsite brewing facilities and outsourced part of the brewing to companies in Syracuse and Saratoga Springs. And in 1999, the company began selling is nutty malt ale in bottles, while continuing to distribute its kegs so bars throughout New York State can serve the popular beer on draught.

Sales gradually began to climb as the beer joined the ranks of other Northeastern-brewed mainstream brands (Samuel Adams) and microbrews (Honey Brown). While the company grew exponentially, it began to depend on its bottled beer to decide where it was going next. Sackets Harbor established lofty sales goals—93,000 gallons of beer a year, about double what it was currently selling—to justify building a new brewery in the Watertown, New York, area.

REASON FOR REDESIGN
To help meet this goal, Sackets Harbor wanted to refresh its current packaging with a few simple changes, to build a little excitement among its current consumers. However, when it contacted its former design firm, Sackets Harbor learned the vendor had since gone out of business—taking the original files with them.

The company approached Iron Design for help. Together, the creative team and the client realized the situation was a blessing in disguise: It was an unanticipated opportunity to reevaluate the micro-brewer's brand.

The previous label, designed in line with the beer's name, used a historical painting of the Battle of 1812 as its main thematic device and generally appealed to an older demographic of beer enthusiasts. After extensive research, as well as informal market testing of competing beers, the creative team suggested positioning the beer as a contemporary alternative to mainstream competing ales and targeting a slightly younger consumer to meet sales objectives. Therefore, the new label needed to be more contemporary looking while retaining elements of the historic look to reinforce the brand.

REDESIGN OBJECTIVES
- Infuse modern elements into War of 1812 Ale's historic-looking label to appeal to younger consumers
- Strike a balance between a distinctly local microbrew, with nods to New York history, and a beer as appealing to the mainstream as the ale's well-known competitors
- Create a label exciting enough to help Sackets Harbor Brewing sell more bottled beer and, ultimately, achieve its aggressive sales goals

THE RESULTS
Retailers and consumers have been very receptive to the new look. As part of the sell, Iron Design also designed an 1812 Light, scheduled for release soon, companion twelve-packs and cases, as well as redesigned tap handles for the bars that serve War of 1812 Ale on draught, so consumers can establish a visual link between the beer they drink in the bar and the bottles they see on the store shelves.

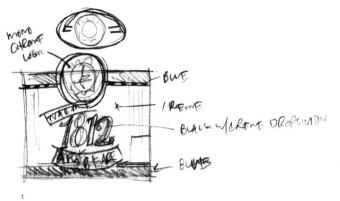

1

2

3

4

5

6

7

8

9

1, 2
Designers looked for ways to make the label more contemporary and appealing to younger consumers while still giving the appropriate nod to the established brand, which was grounded in history. Early sketches explore the idea of playing up the "1812"—the most memorable part of the brand's name—while still retaining the historic symbolism, namely the beer's trademark warship.

3
Because the redesign provided an opportunity for Sackets Harbor to take chances with its brand, designers' early comps ran the gamut from mock-ups that maintained the spirit of the original label to ideas that were a little more daring. This comp ventured only a few steps from the original, playing up the existing label's colonial ship.

4
A second comp used rough, bold letters with gritty static—a masculine, rock-and-roll logo stamped over a less obvious rendering of the ship.

5
Still another comp blended sophisticated type and illustration with a historical feel, capped off by the slogan "Sip a Bit of History" inscribed on the neckband.

6, 7
The client selected this final direction, a layered comp using patterned drop shadows and experimental type.

8, 9
The designers then took this approach and ran with it, rendering bleeding colors, random illustration patterns, and varied type for a label with noise and energy. The bottle brought War of 1812 Ale's origins into the new millennium with the catchy slogan "History never tasted so good."

Somerfield

DESIGN
TAXI Studios, Bristol, United Kingdom
MARKET
United Kingdom

before

An informal study of fresh soup lines at a number of other U.K. supermarkets demonstrated that many were doing similar things graphically. Like the Somerfield soups, they tended to use natural colors and prominent photographs of the soups' ingredients. Somerfield's creative firm, TAXI Studios, resolved to take a different approach to help the private-label fresh soups stand out from the crowd.

The Somerfield soup cartons that launched were striking, with a shock of white scrawled across a pitch-black label. The whimsical chalkboard-style writing, however, keeps the impression friendly instead of severe. Intricately detailed and colorful illustrations of the soup's ingredients brighten up the package and create an easy-to-decipher system for the many different flavors.

Somerfield Design Process

Somerfield, with nearly 1,300 supermarkets and convenience stores across the United Kingdom, specializes in fresh, organic foods "made easy," offering many reheatable options for busy consumers. One of these offerings is a line of private-label fresh soups in the refrigerated section—easy to heat in the microwave and eat immediately. With flavors such as chicken and vegetable, pea and ham, minestrone, and broccoli and Stilton, the soups promise hearty, healthy meals with a fresh taste and quality ingredients.

REASON FOR REDESIGN

Somerfield's soups competed directly with fresh soups with strong brand names, such as the New Covent Garden Food Co. The company wanted to find a way to boost consumer sales of the soups. Somerfield also needed to find a way to reduce waste. The soup was packaged in plastic bags, which often broke during shipping, wasting a great deal of product and driving up production costs. The bags also became extremely hot when consumers microwaved them, posing safety problems for customers.

Somerfield charged TAXI Studios with rethinking the soup containers. TAXI designers visited a number of prominent U.K. supermarkets to evaluate their fresh soup packages and were surprised to find an unfilled niche. "The conclusion was that everyone was copying each other's designs," says TAXI's Spencer Buck. "No one had understood that there was an opportunity to do something different. So we did."

REDESIGN OBJECTIVES

- Compete directly with major brands of fresh soup packaging by launching a unique new approach
- Create a packaging system to help promote the freshness and quality of the soups, thereby increasing sales
- Transfer the soups to more practical plastic tubs rather than bags to make them safer, more convenient, and more appealing to consumers

THE RESULTS

The supermarket chain rallied behind the newly rebranded soups. Outside of the retail environment, they earned some attention as well—the new packaging won a number of awards, including the London International Advertising Awards, One Show Design, *Adline* Magazine's Cream Award, and the F.A.B. International Food & Beverage Creative Excellence Awards.

1

2

3

4

5

6

7

1
At the same time as the redesign, the designers set out to rethink Somerfield soups' structural packaging, because the bags were inconvenient and ineffective. TAXI proposed plastic tubs or cartons, which would prevent spillage and would be safer when heated. They were also more contemporary and interesting looking than the bags.

2–4
Rather than focusing on the literal meaning of freshness with real photos of products, the designers looked at "fresh" from a different perspective. In initial sketches, they played with the idea of skewed hand-writing displaying the product name and details, with tiny depictions of the soup's ingredients underneath. This was a casual approach that communicated freshness as an attitude more than a physical state.

5
In the next phase, the design became white chalk writing and sketches on a blackboard, giving the design an even more free-form, youthful feeling.

6, 7
Expanding on the blackboard idea, the artists then began incorporating color. Different ideas included detailed drawings of the ingredients rendered in chalk.

Xerox

DESIGN
Dunn and Rice Design, Rochester, New York
CREATIVE DIRECTOR
John Dunn
MARKET
Worldwide

before

Despite Xerox's unassailable brand, packaging for the company's paper and specialty media products wasn't unified on the store shelf. From product to product, the wrapping could look radically different—a spectrum of typefaces, colors, and illustrations. The pixelated treatment of the "digital" Xerox *X* also subtracted from the corporate logo's impact and distanced the paper from other Xerox products. The Xerox Supplies Business Group wanted a more consistent application of the Xerox brand to help the products stand out from the competition.

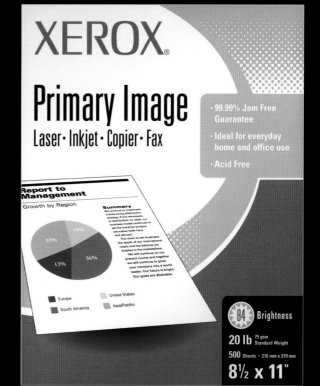

In the final packaging design, a swoosh of specific product colors intersects an image representing a customer application for that paper variety. The visual impact of the design, the consistent placement of the corporate logo and product information typefaces, and the use of eye-catching colors—including the corporate PMS red—all help Xerox break through the marketing clutter.

Xerox Design Process

Xerox is one of the strongest and most recognized brands in the world, on par with brands such as Coca-Cola, Disney, and Sony. But as often happens with companies that have a growing and diverse range of products, Xerox's brand internally took on a life of its own, so that the different divisions of the company interpreted it in very different ways.

Such was the case with the Xerox Supplies Group. The packaging of Xerox's comprehensive line of paper, specialty media, and consumable products was widely disparate and had become dated in the marketplace. Different packaging designs, carton materials, logos, and color treatments created an inconsistent brand experience with the customer.

REASON FOR REDESIGN

Despite the strong overall brand position held by Xerox Corp., Xerox paper and specialty media products no longer maintained a strong differentiation on retail shelves already crowded with prominent brands. The design was no longer helping Xerox stay competitive in the market, and the brand was weakened when portrayed so many different ways through the packaging.

REDESIGN OBJECTIVES

- Strengthen brand representation on product packaging
- Simplify and clarify messaging about Xerox paper and consumables
- Unify all Xerox supplies products under a single worldwide architecture

THE RESULTS

The redesign has helped Xerox achieve its ultimate goal: to preserve retail shelf space and rebuild brand awareness, according to Steve Simpson, vice president of Xerox Supplies Business Group.

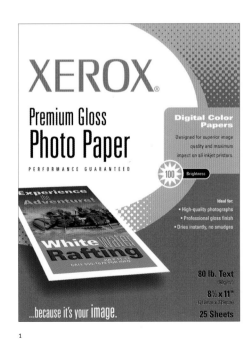

1

2

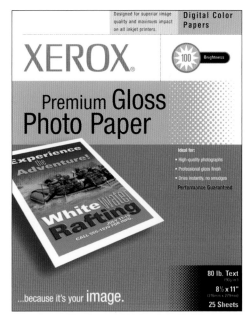

3

4

1, 2
In initial concepts, designers experimented with building an architecture that could support each variety of paper, using the Xerox corporate brand color, PMS 032, as the foundation for each mock-up. Responding to focus group feedback, designers incorporated renderings of images printed on featured papers to show the product in use. The digital concept, removed from the logo, continue to survive in the dots.

3, 4
Focus groups responded that the product information was most effective when prominently featured consistently across the packaging system as white type in black boxes. They also told the creative team that the tagline incorporated in the mock-ups, "... because it's your image," didn't add value to the overall brand.

5
Xerox Supplies then applied the elements used in paper and specialty media packaging to the wide array of Xerox consumable product cartons. Now cartons of toner, dry ink, print cartridges, or developers clearly appear to come from the same company. The swoosh, the placement of the corporate logo, the typeface, and the consistent use of black and Xerox red on cartons bring a unified design approach to Xerox packaging. Worldwide, Xerox customers now have a consistent brand experience.

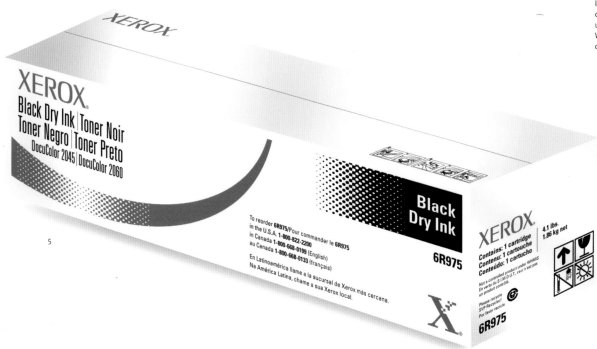

5

Directory

Addis Group, Inc.
28
2515 Ninth Street
Berkeley, CA 94710
United States
510-704-7500
www.addis.com

Avon
92
1251 Avenue of the Americas
New York, NY 10020
United States
212-282-7000
www.avoncompany.com

Bamboo
118
119 North Fourth Street, #503
Minneapolis, MN 55401
United States
612-332-7100
www.bamboo-design.com

Blackburn's Design
142
16 Carlisle Street
London W1D 3BT, England
United Kingdom
44-20-7734-7646
www.blackburndesign.com

Chute Gerdeman
114
455 South Ludlow Alley
Columbus, OH 43215
United States
614-469-1001
www.chutegerdeman.com

cincodemayo
68
5 de mayo 1058 pte.
Monterrey, N.L.
64000
Mexico
52-81-8342-5242
www.cincodemayo.to

Cross Colours
74
8 Eastwood Road
Dunkeld West 2196
Johannesburg
South Africa
27-11-442-2080
www.crosscolours.co.za

Curiosity, Inc.
73, 122
2-45-7 Honmachi
Shibuya-ku
Tokyo 151-0071
Japan
81-3-5333-8525
www.curiosity.co.jp

Dunn and Rice Design
154
16 North Goodman Street #100
Rochester, NY 14607
United States
800-677-2075
www.dunnandrice.com

Fitch:London
56
121-141 Westbourne Terrace
London, W2 6JR, England
United Kingdom
44-20-7479-0900
www.fitch.com

**Hornall Anderson
Design Works**
82
1008 Western Avenue
Suite 600
Seattle, WA 98104
United States
206-826-2329
www.hadw.com

Ideas Frescas
20, 38
Edificio Eben Ezer, Tercer Nivel,
Boulevard Sur, Santa Elena,
Antiguo Cuscatlan
El Salvador
503-248-7420
www.ideas-frescas.com

Ingalls & Associates
42
10 Arkansas Street, Suite E
San Francisco, CA 94109
United States
415-626-6395
tom@ingallsdesign.com

Interbrand
110
130 Fifth Avenue
New York, NY 10011
United States
212-798-7626
www.interbrand.com

Iron Design
146
120 North Aurora Street
Suite 5A
Ithaca, NY 14850
United States
607-275-9544
www.irondesign.com

Karacters Design Group
34, 132
1600 777 Hornby Street
Vancouver, British Columbia
Canada V6Z 2T3
604-640-4327
www.karacters.com

Lee Design Studio
64
5801 Ostrom Avenue
Encino, CA 91316
United States
818-881-3919

Lippa Pearce
141
358A Richmond Road
Twickenham TW1 2DU, England
United Kingdom
44-20-8744-2100
www.lippapearce.com

LMS Design
100, 128
2 Stamford Landing
Stamford, CT 06902
United States
203-975-2500
www.lmsdesign.com

MOD/Michael Osborne Design
60, 109
444 De Haro Street, Suite 207
San Francisco, CA 94107
United States
415-255-0125
www.modsf.com

One Zero Charlie
33, 104
5112 Greenwood Road
Greenwood, IL 60097
United States
815-648-4591
www.onezerocharlie.net

Parham Santana
96
7 West 18th Street
New York, NY 10011
United States
212-645-7501
www.parhamsantana.com

Pearlfisher
16
12 Addison Avenue
London, W11 4QR, England
United Kingdom
44-20-7603-8666
www.pearlfisher.com

PrimoAngeli:Fitch
12
101 15th Street
San Francisco, CA 94103
United States
415-551-1900
www.primo.com

Proteus Design
86
77 North Washington Street
8th Floor
Boston, MA 02114
United States
617-263-2211
www.proteusdesign.com

SooHoo Designers
136
1424 Marcelina Avenue
Torrance, CA 90501
United States
310-381-0170
www.soohoodesign.com

Sussner Design Company
78
212 3rd Avenue, Suite 505
Minneapolis, MN 55401
United States
612-339-2886
www.sussner.com

TAXI Studio
150
Abbots Leigh
Bristol BS8 3RA, England
United Kingdom
44-114-973-5151
www.taxistudio.co.uk

TD2
109
Ibsen 43, 8th Floor
Col. Polanco 11560
Mexico
51-55-5281-6999
www.td2.com.mx

Tesser
50
650 Delancey Street
Loft 404
San Francisco, CA 94107
United States
415-541-1999
www.tesser.com

Wallace Church
24
330 E. 48 Street
New York, NY 10017
United States
212-755-2903
www.wallacechurch.com

Wink
46
417 First Avenue North
Minneapolis, MN 55401
United States
612-630-5139
www.wink-mpls.com

Xerox Corporation
154
800 Long Ridge Road
Stamford, CT 06904
United States
203-968-3000
www.xerox.com

About the Author

Stacey King Gordon is a writer and editor in the San Francisco Bay Area. She is a frequent contributor to *HOW* magazine and the author of *Magazine Design That Works* (Rockport, 2001).

www.night-writer.com